THE NOVELIST
AND THE PASSION STORY

THE NOVELIST
AND THE
PASSION STORY

F. W. DILLISTONE, D.D.

DEAN OF LIVERPOOL

STATE COLLEGE
LIBRARY

FRAMINGHAM, MASS.

COLLINS
ST JAMES'S PLACE, LONDON
1960

TO
FRANCIS NEILSON
WITH ADMIRATION AND
GRATITUDE

© F. W. DILLISTONE, 1960
PRINTED IN GREAT BRITAIN
COLLINS CLEAR-TYPE PRESS : LONDON AND GLASGOW

ACKNOWLEDGMENTS

The author and publishers wish to acknowledge their indebtedness for permission to use copyright material contained in this volume as follows: From *Shorter Collected Poems, 1930-1944* by W. H. Auden, published by Messrs. Faber & Faber Ltd.: from *Writers At Work* (1958), edited by Malcolm Cowley, published by Messrs. Secker & Warburg Ltd.: from *A Fable* by William Faulkner, published by Messrs. Chatto & Windus, London and Random House, New York: from *Aspects of the Novel* by E. M. Forster, published by Messrs. Edward Arnold & Co.: from *Christ Recrucified* by Nikos Kazantzakis, published by Messrs. Bruno Cassirer Ltd.: from *The Lamb* and *The Dark Angels* by Francois Mauriac, published by Messrs. Eyre & Spottiswoode Ltd.: from *Time and The Novel* by A. A. Mendilow, published by Peter Nevill Ltd.

CONTENTS

PREFACE

DURING THE course of my visit to Lincoln to deliver the passiontide lectures at the Bishop's Hostel in 1958, I had the opportunity of being present at the performance of the St. Matthew Passion in the Minster. To participate in Bach's interpretation of the Passion through music seems an entirely natural thing to do. Similarly to expose oneself to a great artist's interpretation of the Passion through colour and line and form would also seem a very normal procedure. I am not sure, however, that one would quite so readily turn to a novelist for such an interpretation though it is clear that he, like his fellow artists, has often been fascinated by the critical event of Calvary and has sought, through his story, to disclose its inner meaning to its readers.

In a variety of ways I became interested in the novelist's use of the Passion-story and it seemed to me a theme worthy to be explored within the Lincoln Series. My suggestion was warmly welcomed by the Warden, Dr. Oliver Tomkins (now Bishop of Bristol), and I am deeply indebted to him, to his Staff and to the Students for their ready interest in what I had to report from my own adventures into unfamiliar territory. I still recall with great pleasure my discussions with those whom I

9

found deeply concerned about the problem of communicating the Gospel through forms which can be vivid and compelling within our contemporary world.

CHAPTER I

THE PASSION STORY TO-DAY

IT WAS the first Sunday after Easter. Her Majesty's Judges of Assize, robed in scarlet and ermine, attended morning service in the cathedral where they were surrounded by the dignity proper to those responsible for the administration of the law. The triumphant notes of Bach's Easter Music, the joy of the well-known Easter Hymns, the impressive argument of a well-ordered sermon—all added to the impressiveness of the occasion. But at the heart of everything, to some perhaps the most memorable part of the whole ceremony, was a simple story read by the Sheriff's Chaplain. It was the story of two who walked from Jerusalem to Emmaus and were joined by a third: and of the things that happened by the way, and how he was known of them in the breaking of the bread.

This story, told and re-told, read and re-read times without number, translated into virtually every language of mankind, analysed, interpreted, applied in every kind of circumstance, still retains its astonishing power to interest, to illuminate, to inspire. The events happened more than 1900 years ago, but through the story they become entirely contemporary. The movement of the story corresponds, we know, to the movement of human life everywhere and it is always possible that the goal towards which the story leads may find its counterpart within the circumstances of a wholly different age.

The Sunday morning service had ended and the Judges had departed. Three friends were re-arranging the seating in the Cathedral when a member of the Chapter who was passing by turned to exchange words with them. A reference to a common interest straightway reminded him of a story and at once the age-long pattern was being re-enacted in a new context—the story-teller with his audience of two or three, recounting with all the powers at his command an unusual episode which he had observed and in which to a small degree he had been involved. He told of an organised robbery carried out on a public holiday in broad daylight with tourists coming and going and scarcely noticing the unusual transference of commodities from a stationary lorry to an attendant taxi— an exploit containing elements of ingenuity and daring— and still more perhaps of comedy—through its effortless hoodwinking of all, including the story-teller, who might have taken action to prevent its success. The narrator hurried through the original sequence, his hearers were caught up within the living movement and while the story lasted, all could share a certain exhilarating awareness of travelling together towards a common goal.

So on one day, in two different contexts, two quite different kinds of stories were being told. The story of wondering surprise in a far-off land long ago, the story of comic surprise in a nearby situation only six days previously. But this in fact was no unusual day. For man, as such, is an inveterate story-teller and the human imagination as such has ever delighted to receive the good story whether through the spoken or the written word. Stories of heroes and adventurers, of leaders and kings, of love and hatred, of nobility and shame—all find a receptive ear so long as they are related to the authentic movement of human life.

It is true that at different periods of human history the story has assumed different forms. One age delights in the saga, another in the myth, another in the epic, another in the parable: or again one period is specially productive of tribal history, another of individual history, another of world history. Not that any hard and fast distinction can be drawn between the conventions of one age and those of another but the forms most popular in any particular society can readily be recognised. There can be little doubt for example that in the Western world of the past two centuries two forms have come to occupy an almost unchallenged position as the two most suitable for the containing and expressing of the stories of mankind. They are what I might call the reliable history and the authentic novel.

If the story purports to recount the history of the past it must give the most careful attention to the evidence provided by the various available witnesses to the past—inscriptions, documents, archæological remains, language-forms—and only when it is evident that a story-teller of past events has dealt faithfully with the evidence at his disposal can he be sure of a hearing. The history which is " cooked " or " slanted " or " biased " may win a temporary success but the general judgment of the democratic West has been against this kind of story. Only a story true to what is called the factual evidence is in the long run acceptable.

If on the other hand the story is of the order of fiction, it must deal faithfully with the evidence provided by the various witnesses to the abiding structures of individual and social life—to the writings of welfare workers and social scientists, to the testimonies which come from individual observation and analysis of experience. The novelist who makes his imaginary characters talk and act in ways which are quite remote from anything that belongs to life as we know it may gain a temporary following from those who are seeking entertainment or escape from the world of reality but again the general judgment of the democracies has been against this type of fiction. The novel is meant to set us back from life so that we may see it in better perspective and with a fuller range of understanding. There must be an authentic corres- pondence between the life situations of the novel and those of ordinary human existence if its story is to succeed in stimulating and pleasing and finally satisfying its readers.

II

Here then we find two common forms—the history and the novel—in which in the past two centuries the *story* has normally taken shape. Reliable stories of the past together with authentic stories of the present have constituted the larger part of the Western world's reading and its libraries are crammed with the work of its story-tellers. What place then in this vast accumulation can be found for the story which is central to the Christian faith, and which it has been the responsibility of Christian witnesses to tell at all times and in all places by every means in their power? One answer is obvious. To tell the story as reliable history has been the task and concern of innumerable preachers, teachers and writers since the beginning of the historical era at the turn of the eighteenth century. No pains have been spared to ensure that every detail of the story has been tested and checked and examined and that the record of the life and passion and death of Jesus as told to-day shall be entitled to be regarded as reliable history.

But what of the novel? *Can* the novelist relate himself in any significant way to the Passion Story? Is it not his concern, as I have already suggested, to tell us stories which are true to human life as he sees it to-day? How then can he use material which comes from a far-a-way past and which seems in so many ways unrelated to the contemporary scene? So far as I can judge two major possibilities are open to him.

The first is to focus the reader's attention on the past and to write an avowedly historical novel. He sets to work to avail himself of the best results of historical scholarship and thereby places his story firmly in the geographical, political, economic and social setting of the Mediterranean world of the first century. The daily life of the citizen of the Roman Empire and more especially that of a Galilean peasant forms itself in his imagination and the causes of tension between Jew and Jew as well as between Jew and Roman become increasingly familiar to him. As the general picture of life in Jerusalem and Galilee gradually takes shape he is ready to pass on to the next stage—the mastery of the particular history of Jesus of Nazareth.

It seems to me that the critical events of this history have now been established beyond any reasonable possibility of doubt and the novelist is virtually bound to relate his story to them. But so long as he allows them to act as guide-posts for the onward movement of his story his imagination can range as widely as he pleases as he attempts to relate other characters to the central historical figure. An extraordinarily varied assortment of human types is already to be found in the evangelists' own stories: Peter, Judas, The Beloved Disciple, Caiaphas, Pilate, The Soldiers, Thomas, Barabbas. But there is nothing to prevent the novelist from adding to this company in any way he believes to be authentic and appropriate and thereby throwing light on more aspects of ordinary human experience.

In a very real sense the innumerable attempts that have been made during the past century to write the life of Christ can be classed as historical novels. Few have deviated from the path laid out by the critical turning-points of which the Gospels tell us—the Call, the Temptation, the preaching of the Kingdom, the Opposition culminating in the Passion and the Death—but every writer has recounted the life in his own particular way. It is an imaginary construction. At the same time the more he has been able to enter into the life of first-century Palestine and the more he has succeeded in making the figure of Jesus stand out as real and compelling within that particular situation the more efficient he has been in the performance of his task.

But the usual practice has been to reserve the title " novelist " for one who does not restrict himself to the recorded sayings and incidents of the New Testament but freely invents characters and situations in order to make the whole story more fresh and exciting to his readers. The earliest readers of the Gospel stories possessed a first-hand knowledge of places and events denied to us. So easily, then, the narratives fail to make their proper impact upon us because we are unaware of all the things which the writer took for granted in the background experience of his readers. It is the historical novelist's aim to bring some, at least, of these hidden assumptions to expression through the behaviour of significant characters introduced into the story. If they can talk and act in such a way that we who read can find ourselves transported back into the first-century environment and can there encounter Jesus and His disciples afresh and see them related to people who impress us as real and belonging to their time, then the whole effect can be to extend our understanding of the meaning of His mission and to relate His impact on a past age directly to our own.

Examples of the historical novel in which the figure of Jesus of Nazareth plays the central part are many. But few have been entirely successful. The constant dilemma has been that the more the novelist succeeds in making Jesus a child of his own time, the less related he seems to be to our present condition. The more evidently he belongs to the social tensions and political cross-currents of first-century Palestine, the less evident is his significance for the world of the twentieth century. And the very success of the delineation of imaginary characters can all too easily obscure the central character whose essential features are already given in the Gospel record.

Perhaps the best known of recent attempts to focus attention upon the mission of Jesus through the medium of the historical novel has been Lloyd Douglas's book *The Robe*. Of the deep sincerity and devotion of the author there can be no question. To the popular appeal which such a presentation makes, both the wide distribution of the book and the phenomenal success of the subsequent film bear eloquent testimony. But the device by which the author seeks to magnify the significance of Jesus by focusing on the robe which he wore is a questionable one. And the overall effect of the novel is to extend our knowledge of life in Caesar's empire rather than to deepen our understanding of God's revelation in Christ. The world which the novelist depicts is fascinating but remote. Such things may well have happened *then*. They do not happen *now*. The career of Jesus can be fitted into the past. It has little bearing upon present experience. Such is the danger. It threatens the work of the professional historian as well as that of the historical novelist when the subject is Jesus of Nazareth. The very brilliance of the historical reconstruction may stand in the way of an actual encounter with the living Christ.

While allowing, then, that the historical novel is a legitimate form for the artist to employ in his attempt to present Jesus and His relationships vividly before the eyes of his contemporaries, I doubt if it is the best. It is, perhaps, most effective at a period in history when the main features of social life in a particular country approximate closely to those that are known to have characterised the Palestine of 1900 years ago. The contemporary Hungarian novelist, for example, might well succeed in writing a powerful historical novel by interpreting the story of Jesus' mission and suffering and death in the light of the recent tragic experiences of his own country. But even here the reverse process might be still more effective and it is of this second way by which the novelist may use the Passion Story in his writing that I want particularly to write.

III

The second possibility open to the novelist is to write about his contemporary world openly and frankly but with the essential pattern of the Passion narrative forming the inner framework of his own story. It is, of course, impossible for him to do this unless he believes that the successive stages in the recorded life of Jesus do correspond to the general sequence of events which may be traced in the career of every heroic figure who carries out a mission of redemption for his fellow-men. Such a mission may be performed by an individual seeking consciously to follow in the steps of the Christ and to fashion his life after the pattern displayed in the Gospels. But not necessarily so. In dedicating himself to the service of his fellows he may almost unconsciously find himself caught up into a sequence of temporary acceptance, growing opposition,

19

rejection, suffering, dereliction, vindication, strangely similar to that which marked the career of Jesus of Nazareth Himself.

That the appearance of the basic pattern of the Passion in the life-story of an individual heroic figure is not an impossible conception becomes clear enough if we think of some of the great names of Christian history—a Paul, a Francis, a Sadhu Sundar Singh. In the case of Paul the essential pattern of acceptance of God's call, opposition, suffering, renewal of life, had so burned itself into his imagination that he asked for nothing more than that he might so be identified with the Christ in His sufferings that he might also share with Him in the glory of His resurrection. Daily he surrendered himself afresh to the way of the Cross in the faith that the path thus chosen would lead to the breaking forth of a richer and fuller life. " Death worketh in us but life in you." " We which live are constantly being delivered to death for Jesus' sake that the life also of Jesus might be manifested in you."

And this is not simply an exceptional example taken from a period in the far distant past. Nor is it only in the exceptional lives of heroic individuals in the present that this pattern can be seen. I was struck, for instance, in reading a recent review of the life of a man who had occupied no exalted position and was not even well known beyond a fairly limited circle. The reviewer was Bishop Mervyn Haigh and this is his final reflection: " On reading and re-reading the book, some will catch sight of another sequence shining through those of book and life alike—something, that is, of Bethlehem, Nazareth, call at Jordan and testing in the wilderness, ministry in Galilee and in Judaea, journey to Jerusalem, suffering, dereliction, death and—' a door opened in heaven '."*

To catch sight of the pattern of the Passion even in the sequence of a modern biography is therefore entirely possible. How much more is it possible in the novel where the writer's imagination is untrammelled by detailed and often seemingly irrelevant facts and is free to transpose the original and all-important pattern into the setting of his own time. He can expose the clash of characters which is a perennial feature of the human scene and show how the imagined Christ-figure would be treated by His contemporaries of another age: He can so take hold of the critical stages of the Passion Story and weave them into his novel that the reader finds himself acknowledging that here indeed is the authentic pattern and final meaning of the whole manifold variety of human existence.

For what after all is the novel? In his book *Time and the Novel*, Mr. A. A. Mendilow attempts a definition which he admits is a somewhat cumbersome description but it will serve our purpose well enough. " The novel " he writes " is a fictitious narrative in prose which seeks to illustrate and illuminate human experience and behaviour within the limitations imposed by the medium of language and the necessities of form, by approximating as closely as possible to what we apprehend as reality.

" The test of its immediate success is its power to evoke the feeling of presentness (in a double sense) in and at

* Review of *Hugh Compton Warner:* a biography by his widow, Nancy le Plastrier Warner.

that reality; this assumes that the reader will co-operate with the author to the extent of accepting the conventions on which the illusory reality of fiction is based, by yielding to ' the willing suspension of disbelief.'

" Its more lasting value may be estimated, firstly by the degree to which the discriminating reader feels the whole work as a symbol of something wider and deeper than the actual theme, something that sets up in him reverberations that invest the particular human problem treated with universal significance; secondly, if the discriminating reader can recognise in the relations of the parts to one another and to the whole some underlying, formal principle, corresponding so closely to the conception of the theme as to appear inevitable. The theme, the form and the medium of the novel should be but three aspects of something that is one and indivisible—that intangible that we may call the author's vision."*

In each of the novels with which I shall be concerned the " theme " in general terms is the power of redemptive suffering. There is always a central character who is ready to accept suffering and even death in the service of a transcendent value, a worthy end. The formal " principle " is the sequence of events revealed in the Passion Story of the New Testament, a sequence which in that story seems natural and indeed inevitable and which provides a completely authentic framework for the novelist's own story. In every case, I believe, the novel does evoke the feeling of presentness in and at the final reality described so simply and yet so movingly by the Fourth Evangelist: The Lamb of God bearing away the

* p. 238, A. A. Mendilow *Time and the Novel*.

sin of the world. And in every case, I believe, it is possible to see the whole work as a symbol of that widest and deepest of all interpretative ideas: that God was reconciling the world to Himself in Christ.

Of the language medium employed in two of the novels that I have chosen I am not competent to speak. I have no sufficient knowledge of French and none of Modern Greek to enable me to judge whether Mauriac and Kazantzakis have succeeded in finding a vocabulary and style appropriate to the particular theme and form which they have chosen. I think a case could be made for the rightness of the unusual language media employed by Melville and Faulkner but to this I do not propose to make more than incidental reference. My over-riding concern is with the way in which each writer allows the underlying form of the Passion sequence to control his narrative and with the particular interpretation of the working out of the process of divine reconciliation in the universe which each writer gives.

But before beginning a detailed study of individual novelists I want to introduce them as not only important in their own right but as significant representatives of important traditions. From the point of view of numbers, organisation, historical continuity, and international out-reach, the Roman Catholic Church occupies the foremost place in Christendom to-day. But Eastern Orthodoxy can lay claim to an even closer touch with antiquity and to an even firmer hold upon the unchanging forms of early Christianity. It is natural that each of these traditions should be represented in our survey of the Passion Story in modern fiction. The novelist may not feel at ease with all the doctrines and practices of his own communion but even when he is critical he is still standing within the general framework of customs and ideas which belongs to his own tradition.

Outside the boundaries of the Roman and the Orthodox communions it is not easy to discover any simple classification of other Christian bodies. Yet the early distinction which appeared in the sixteenth century between Lutheran and Calvinist proved to be a very significant one for future generations. Calvinism was radical, well organised, theologically dogmatic, held together amidst all variation of nation and class within one intellectual system. Lutheranism on the other hand had more regard for the traditional, the mystical, the dialectical, and was deeply rooted in a particular environment of blood and soil. And in varying forms this latter type of Christian expression has persisted since the Reformation—a tradition without too precise dogmatic definition, giving freedom for individual experimentation though encouraging corporate solidarity, open to new learning though clinging to old forms.

Our other two novelists stand roughly within these two types of Christian outlook. Though in many ways rebelling against the system in which he had been reared, Melville still accepted many of the assumptions of the Calvinism which had formed the intellectual framework of the early New England settlers. And although Faulkner might be surprised to find his name associated with that of Luther yet in a general way he belongs to that mixed Protestant heritage in which the individual and the community, the mystical and the institutional, the sacred and the secular, the new and the old are in constant tension and even conflict.

As a rough classification, then, we can refer to the writers whose novels we are to study as belonging to the Roman, the Orthodox, the Calvinist and the Protestant traditions. They were not originally chosen in order to include these major groupings of Christendom but rather because in each case it became clear that the novelist had composed his book within the structural framework provided by the Passion Story of the Gospels. To examine the work of each writer and to see what light it throws on the meaning of the central redeeming act of the Christian faith is my purpose in the following chapters.

CHAPTER 2

A LAMB TO THE SLAUGHTER

FRANCOIS MAURIAC has been called the greatest living European novelist. Certainly he has claims to be regarded as France's leading Catholic novelist. Since 1920 a steady stream of books—novels, plays, biographies, essays in criticism—has come from his pen and in 1952 he was awarded the Nobel Prize for Literature.

He was born in 1885 in Bordeaux and received his early education in that city. Only after his graduation from the University of Bordeaux did he move to Paris for a brief period of further study. This fact is of some significance as one approaches his novels for he has affirmed that they all take place in the period contemporary with his adolescence and his youth. In other words their setting is that of the provincial society of Southern France in the period before the first great World War. It is a Catholic feudal society whose structure has changed but little from that of medieval times.

Within this relatively constant social structure Mauriac is able to give full play to the tensions and attractions which exist within ordinary human relationships, to the conflicts and struggles which go on within the individual human heart. In particular his own strong Catholic commitment gives him extraordinary insight into the clash between religious principles and duties on the one hand and the desires of the flesh on the other. Through his novels, he says, he tries " to make the Catholic universe of evil perceptible, tangible, odorous. The theologians give us an abstract idea of the sinner. I give him flesh and blood."

Mauriac is quite explicit concerning the Christian foundation and character of his work. " As a novelist," he has said, " I have been engaged only on the religious level. Being a Christian my Christian beliefs dominate my novels, not because I want to make propaganda for Christianity but because it is the deepest part of my nature. I must say . . . that I am a Christian first and last, which means a man who feels himself responsible to God and to his conscience for the epoch that he lives in." This means that even when in Mauriac's stories the surface of life is heaving and swelling and man is being tossed hither and thither by apparently uncontrollable forces, deep down there is the tremendously strong movement of salvation which actually holds all things within its powerful embrace.

The central Christian themes of Sin and Grace are never far away from the author's attention in any of his writings but in one late novel *The Lamb*, the whole process of redemption is dramatically represented through the career of an obvious Christ-figure. Here in the setting of European feudal society we see a lamb bearing the load of that society's sins. Published in 1954, the novel came late in Mauriac's career but with its unmistakable background of the Passion Story it brings to a focus its author's convictions about the power of suffering and sacrifice to bring healing and reconciliation to mankind.

II

One of the best known of Mauriac's earliest novels is *A Woman of the Pharisees*. In this book the central figure is a certain Brigitte Pian, a devoted daughter of the Church, punctilious in the observance of religious obligations and in the performance of works of mercy, convinced of her own mission to be a guide to the weak and ignorant, yet eaten up with jealousy, pride, self-righteousness and even cruelty. Chiefly through the sufferings of a priest, M. Calou, the Divine salvation touches her and the final paragraph of the book leaves her in the presence of the Great Compassion, recognising that it is not her frantic attempts to repay her Lord's debts that really matters but rather her response of love to the infinite charity of God.

In this story a boy, Jean de Mirbel, and a girl, Michele Pian, play a prominent part. Jean is the headstrong, selfish son of a tyrannical father and a profligate mother. The final shock which comes from the discovery of his mother's real character nearly ruins him: the love which he gives and receives in his relationship with Michele is the only human factor which restrains him. Even though these two are ultimately brought together as man and wife, it is all too plain that the unhappy legacy of Jean's earlier years will not be easily resolved.

28

The tragic events of *The Lamb* become the more understandable when set against the background of the earlier story. As Mauriac himself writes in a short preface:

" All that is strange, perhaps even monstrous in the man of thirty who, in *The Lamb* bears the name of Jean de Mirbel will seem less strange to those who remember the years of his youth as I described them in *A Woman of the Pharisees*."

A young man Xavier, innocent and unblemished, is in fact caught in the thicket of the jealousies and intrigues growing out of the earlier situation and is ultimately sacrificed on behalf of those whose lives could be redeemed in no other way.

As the story opens, Xavier Dartigelongue has just boarded the train for Paris where he is to enter the Carmelite Seminary. While waiting for the moment of departure, he notices a couple—man and woman—standing together on the platform. They are obviously ill at ease. The man is sullen and impatient to go: the woman is frustrated, appealing, on the verge of tears. The man's seat, it proves, is opposite to Xavier's and before the train reaches Paris the intending Seminarian has become interested, involved and even imprisoned within the circle of the family life of the de Mirbels. He has been brought to believe that only his own intervention in the way dictated by Jean can save the marriage from irretrievable disaster. Postponing his entry into the Seminary he returns the next day with Jean to the family house at Larjuzon.

Arriving there he discovers that Michele is not alone as

29

he had expected. The other occupants of the household are Brigitte Pian who had come on a visit accompanied by a young girl Dominique whom she calls her secretary. In addition there is a small boy Roland, ten years of age, a foundling who is on trial, as it were, for a possible adoption by the de Mirbels, but is already loathed and detested by Jean. His only desire is to get rid of the child as quickly as possible.

The stage is thus set for the working out of a tragic drama. Jean is gripped by a demoniac passion to possess Xavier entirely; Brigitte has an almost similar possessive passion towards Dominique; Michele has a certain womanly interest in both Xavier and Roland; Roland finds in Dominique's understanding and sympathy the one spar to which he can cling from the midst of the ocean of misery in which he is engulfed. These are the relatively settled structures of relationship. But all are suddenly and violently disturbed by the meeting of Xavier and Dominique. Simply and naturally and without reservation they discover their love for one another, a love which goes out freely to others but which immediately creates a fury of jealousy and resentment in those possessed by other desires.

The plot is quite simple. Jean has little difficulty in persuading Madame Pian that she should remove her " secretary " from the place of temptation as soon as possible. The departure provokes a crisis in the behaviour of Roland who sees his only consolation being snatched cruelly away. But Roland's plight calls out all the compassion in Xavier's heart and leads him, in spite of Jean's bitter jealousy, to do everything in his power for the wretched boy. To rescue him he sets out on what proves to be literally a *via dolorosa*. It brings him intense physical and mental suffering but it also brings to fuller revelation the purity and selflessness of his character. He succeeds in restoring Roland to the only one who will care for him and love him before he meets his own death in an accident.

The precise nature of the accident remains a mystery. Jean is the driver of the car and Xavier is the rider of the bicycle. " No one knows whether he threw himself in front of the car on purpose or whether he was blinded by the headlights." But whatever may have been the final cause of the death its immediate effect is to shock Jean and Michele into a completely new awareness of themselves in relation to God. They are purged, transformed, saved. And Xavier " has entered into the possession of Him whom he loved."

III

The altogether significant actions of this drama take place within the familiar setting of the unchanging countryside. The parting at the railway station and the encounter within the railway carriage are important but any form of transportation could have served the author's purpose of bringing two lives together in the circumstances of a shared journey. The city is briefly introduced but chiefly as the place of easy indulgence. Even in Biblical times the city was so regarded. The dim, remote influence of the city may occasionally be felt but the real focus of interest is the country house with its feudal tradition, the garden and the stream, the comfortable domestic surroundings, the village church and its pastor, the family and the child.

This is a setting which is capable not only of evoking nostalgic memories and attractive associations in the minds of many novel-readers but also of expressing much that is most appealing in the European Catholic tradition. Over the past millennium the Catholic Church has related itself closely to the ordinary life of the land, to the estate-owner and the farmer and the peasant, to the cycle of sowing and reaping, birth and death, summer and winter, to the succession of the generations, to the hierarchical structure of feudal society. It is a stable situation, broad-based on the regularities and continuities of nature and it has been the function of the Church to exercise a paternal watch over this whole order of things, establishing discipline, correcting offences, providing unity and continuity within society itself.

In such a structure history is of little account. The events in *The Lamb* can be dated as having taken place in 1921 soon after the war. But they might as well have happened at any time in the last 500 years. Events in the wider world are irrelevant to the drama of personal relationships which is being worked out within the circumscribed domestic scene. The all important influences there, are those of nature not of history—those which play upon the immediate physical senses rather than those which are mediated through social revolution and technological change.

Mauriac himself is a master in the art of evoking vivid

sensual images through his writing. He first recaptures the sense-perceptions of his youth and then expresses them—sounds, sights, even smells—through his words. We feel the mustiness of the bedroom allotted to Xavier. " There was no getting away from the smell of damp-mould, from the old mattress, from the bedside rug, the feel of which was under his knees, the threadbare surface before his eyes. A moth staggered about on the marble top of the chest-of-drawers. The curtains bellied moment-arily in the night-wind, then came to rest. The moth seemed to have settled. The faint sound he heard came from the torn wallpaper moving in the wind." We get a vivid visual impression of the repulsive child—the small, sickly boy with big bulbous head: the snivelling urchin, all tears and snot: the weakly nameless scrap of humanity for which " Xavier gave up all he had to hope for of earthly happiness." We have no difficulty in sharing Michele's emotions about the " torn lumps of blood-stained wool " which had been Xavier's socks.

" The best thing to do it occurred to her would be to bury them in the park. A light drizzle was falling. Though the grass was soaking wet she made her way to the ditch in the meadow. She had a perfectly clear image in her mind of the spot in which she would get rid of her burden —the place where she had seen Xavier squatting with Roland at the water's edge, looking at tadpoles. There was a clump of water-fern nearby. She pulled up a few tufts of grass, laid the parcel in the damp earth, and marked the spot with a stone, as she used to do when she was a child, after burying a broken doll or a dead bird."

This keenness of physical sensation is characteristic of

Catholic writers. It links itself naturally with the attitude which experiences the spiritual intensely in and through the mediation of the physical. When Xavier received the Blessed Sacrament " he savoured it, folded himself about it that nothing of it might be lost! " So the gift comes from God's side. But equally from man's side the offering must find some physical expression. In *The Dark Angels* Mauriac makes one of his characters write " What does ' loving God ' mean? An emotional impulse directed to an entity!—why the very idea is unthinkable. Loving is an act that involves the flesh." In the physical and through the physical the commerce between God and man takes place.

These then are the simplest and most obvious parts of the structure of Mauriac's novels. A feudal society group attached to a traditional plot of land: a relative in-difference to history and to the influence of world forces: a concentration upon the physical senses as mediators of spiritual reality: and within this setting the interplay of human lives, attracting and repelling, loving and hating, seeking to suck in, seeking to pour out. But within this general structure the most important of all forces is at work: the Divine Grace is for ever striving for the salvation of mankind.

IV

What then is the wider theological framework within which Mauriac's characters live and move? There is a revealing passage in the book *Writers at Work* in which

Mauriac declares: " I don't observe and I don't describe; I re-discover. I re-discover the narrow Jansenist world of my devout, unhappy and introverted childhood. It is as though when I was twenty a door within me had closed for ever on that which was going to be the material of my work."

And in *A Woman of the Pharisees* the narrator remarks at one point: " There are, to-day, few Christians, however devout, who recourse to the Eucharist as often as they might. Forty years ago a spirit of fear and trembling still ruled the minds of certain persons in their relations with the Incarnate Love, who, so they had been taught by Jansenism to believe, was implacable."

Quite clearly Mauriac is re-acting sharply against the narrow Jansenist atmosphere of his youth and yet, as is so often the case, the man who reacts still moves within the general framework which he criticises and even attacks at certain points. It may be suggested that Mauriac exposes the excesses and rigidities of Jansenism while at the same time he retains certain of its doctrinal emphases.

What then have been the peculiar features of Jansenism? It has represented in French Catholicism a combination of the predestinarian doctrine of Augustine with the inflexible ethic of Puritanism. What Calvinism came to imply in the world of Protestantism, Jansenism came to denote in the world of Catholicism. At one point indeed, Mauriac, in referring to his own favourite doctrine of redemption through human suffering, makes one of his characters say that it was Calvin who deprived men of this hope. The whole emphasis of Jansen in agreement with Calvin was upon the predestinating activity of God rather than upon any co-operating activity on the part of man. And Mauriac is intent upon breaking out from any narrow determinism or any moral separatism. He must find a due place for man's freedom —freedom to sin, freedom to suffer, freedom to respond to the Divine salvation.

Yet much of the Augustinian framework remains. God is depicted primarily as the supreme overlord, the ruler in whose hands are the destinies of all men and through whose direct control all things are ordered and sustained. It matters not whether one thinks in microcosmic terms of the individual family or in macrocosmic terms of the nation or empire. God is the supreme paternal figure whose concern it is to maintain a proper family order throughout his realm with each individual fulfilling his predestined function and each group occupying its proper status within the larger whole.

The sense of the Divine father-figure is very strong in Mauriac. Man is a child and as such is liable constantly to behave irresponsibly, foolishly, petulantly, obstinately. Yet the hand of God still rests upon him. And in the case of the saint the hand literally compels him to follow a road in the very opposite direction to that to which he himself would incline. " The hand which gripped him so hard he could feel its burning grasp, held him, at times, like a vice so tightly screwed that it was as though the breath was being squeezed out of his body. He was to be pushed along a road where it was past imagination that he could walk." Yet this compulsion is not the compulsion of tyranny but of love. God in the very act of constraining his chosen instrument expresses His own nature through this constraint and shares in the Passion through which the predestined path must lead.

But for those who are not called to the high destiny of sainthood there must be checks, disciplines, punishments. They must never be allowed to disrupt the settled and unchanging Divine order; they must ever be subjected to the forces of attraction which draw men back to their true dependence upon the Divine Father. There must constantly be re-enacted within every situation and circumstance the drama of salvation whereby the Divine in human form bears the load of the sins of erring humanity and brings to men the evidences of the Divine pardon and grace. The world is full of sin but grace overcomes human sin, the grace uniquely revealed in the humiliation and passion of the God-man, Christ Jesus.

Though he delights in the sights and sounds of the natural environment within which his characters live, Mauriac has no illusions about the ugliness and discord which mar their inner lives and relationships. He is particularly aware of the selfishness and jealousies which so often stain the character of the outwardly religious person. Pharisaism is a deadly disease, all too frequently infecting the life of a holy woman. The *Woman of the Pharisees* is like a vampire, sucking the life-blood out of those who surround her, demoniacally possessive, incredibly self-satisfied, seemingly impervious to any appeal for pity and tenderness. In one of the most dramatic interviews of *The Lamb*, Jean accuses Madame Pian of using Dominique solely for her own purposes. " The fact of the matter is " he cries, " that you can't do without her.

She gives you what you want, a bath of young blood, all in the most reputable and spiritual way, of course. I have always thought that the way in which old people like to have the young about them, has something of vampirism about it! "

" Vampirism " she screamed. He could see that she was trembling from head to foot.

A man too, as in the case of Jean de Mirbel, can be jealous and demanding, ever seeking to manipulate others for his own ends. There is a specially revealing sentence in which Jean cries out " I had to have a victim sacrificed for me alone." Here surely is the limit of human selfishness—and it is always possible within the love-relationship. Jean had conceived a real love for Xavier but this love was always trembling on the brink of a fanatical possessiveness. To have Xavier's interest, his concern, his service, even his sacrifice directed solely towards Jean and his ends—this was Jean's consuming desire. It was an attitude which he had revealed in earlier life in his relationship first with his mother, then with the girl who was to be his wife. Now in his contacts with Xavier the attitude becomes an obsession. He would rather kill the object of his attachment than share him with any other human being.

Mauriac never minimises the evil of the human situation. Yet he resists the temptation to despair of men and to write off the human soul as irredeemably bad. He is well aware of the mystery of evil " that mystery at the thought of which Tota's brother (in *The Dark Angels*) had more than once lost heart." Are there human souls that have been given over completely to the Devil? There is so much in human experience to suggest that this is the case. Yet " Alain did not believe that any soul could be given over entirely to ' him '— . . . for, if that were so, then all souls must be in like predicament, because, ever since the Fall, each generation of men had inherited from their forbears enough of evil to ensure their damnation— an obscure madness which, starting far back in the history of the Race, had been embodied in every individual down to those still living—vices kept in chains by some, triumphant in others, coming to rank flower in great-great-nephews."

So Mauriac holds back from any all-embracing predestinarianism. Man is not, as he says elsewhere, an immobile being, fixed, cast in a mould once and for all. He is someone creating himself. He can never remove himself finally and completely from the context of the drama of salvation which is being enacted in the world. There may be the " unending host of prostitutes and pimps, of homo-sexuals and drug-addicts and murderers." But there are also the martyrs and the saints. And men lay upon the saint " all the filthy acts of their own secret lives, and he consents to carry the load." (Said of the Abbé Forcas in *The Dark Angels*.)

v

This is Mauriac's deepest message and it is beautifully expressed in *The Lamb*. For every generation, for every human situation, there must be a lamb if the drama of salvation is to be re-enacted in the setting of a particular place and a particular time. It is true that at one point in history the God-Man was offered in a unique way once and for all. But in Mauriac's view—and here he conforms to the most characteristic strain of Catholic doctrine —it is possible for a saintly Christ-figure at any point of time so to be identified with Christ in character and suffering and sacrifice that he can mediate healing and redemption to the generality of mankind. And this identification is not simply a " spiritual " or emotional impulse directed towards an ideal. It is " an act that involves the flesh." It is a transposition, a transference. It means putting the finger into the print of the nails and thrusting the hand into the side.

It needs little insight to see in Xavier of *The Lamb* such a Christ-figure. His character is defined at the very beginning: " To belong to none that he might belong to all." " I want to take my place with sinners, to be dedicated to their service, handed over to them, saved with them, damned with them." " A counterfeit of the God he loved!—convinced that he must give every scrap of himself to all and each." Xavier is already manifesting the spirit of Him who said when he came into the world " Lo, I come to do Thy will, O my God."

But there is bound to be temptation and testing. The call to turn aside from the chosen path to meet an apparent emergency—is it the call of God or is it the cunning of the Devil? Is the encounter with some obviously needy soul to be classified as " chance " or as a means of becoming integrated into the operation of the Divine Grace? Is the impulse to look into and even to walk into the subterranean hive of human sinfulness to be regarded as the

prompting of the Divine Spirit or of the Enemy of souls?
Xavier knew temptation. For better, for worse, he took
the way of identification.

The Son of Man experiences loneliness, the alienation
of his own family, the misunderstanding of his friends.
Xavier is to pass through similar experiences. He finds
himself at Larjuzon with a sheetless bed and a mattress
smelling of dead mice, " lost and lonely in a hostile house."
Michele accuses him of having " dodged " the Seminary
and of having jumped at an excuse to save him from his
chosen vocation. His mother and father conclude that he
has been turned aside by the wiles of " a man who is the
worst type of libertine." His brother suspects a moral
lapse. His director writes him off as shiftless and in-
curably irresponsible and withdraws from any further
association with him. Xavier finds himself deserted,
exposed, naked as Christ was before being nailed to the
Cross.

But what is partly suggested in the first half of the book
comes to full expression in the second. Xavier is identified
with his Master, body and soul, as he takes upon himself
the burden of the misery of an unwanted and unlovely
boy. This boy, Roland, has found his only solace in the
affection of Dominique and she was being snatched away.
He makes a scene and Jean in his fury throws him into a
darkened room and leaves him there for the night. Xavier
only knows that " not for a single day, a single hour must
he abandon him. Rather than do that he would die.
' Even should the others throw him out neck and crop,
I will faithfully watch over him.' "

He waits till the house is asleep and then, removing his

shoes, he sets off on his *via dolorosa*. A ladder becomes his Cross, too heavy at last to carry and needing to be dragged to its position. His feet are lacerated by the gravel and the pine needles on which he walks. " He moved forward, and at each step he took the wounds on his feet hurt more. He stopped often to change his burden from one shoulder to the other ... It was the very flesh of his body now that was being torn and mangled. In the past he had talked endlessly of the Cross, had fed his meditations on the thought of it, but only here in the loneliness of a cold, dark night, was it borne in upon him that he had never understood its full meaning, had never truly merged himself with the experience. The Cross was not, as he had once believed, a love withdrawn, an agonised bending of the spirit, a humiliation, an obstacle; it was, quite simply, a crushing weight of timber, a bruised and tortured shoulder, carried on feet flayed by stones and earth. Stretching his muscles to the last bearable point, he still moved forward, and thought, as he moved, that he could see before him the thin back of a man. He could see the vertebrae quite clearly, the ribs rising and falling under the thrust of painful breathing, the purple weals of flagellation; the slave of all the ages, the slave eternal."

At last he reaches the child and tries to make his resting-place more comfortable. When the child wakes with a startled cry Xavier comforts him with the words: " It is only I. I am watching beside you." And the child sees him—the torn socks stuck to his feet by blood. " He was little more than a living image of pain. But he belonged to this small creature to whom he was united by a bond which, while life remained would not be loosened, nor after life had gone."

It is a woman, Michele, who rises early and discovers the truth. She sees the blood on the floor, she bathes his wounds, she buries the relics of his saving deed, she understands what he has done. Only Jean remains hard and untouched (though it is true that he has no knowledge of the re-enacted Passion). He is even ready to regard Xavier's love for the boy as an unholy thing, to trample it under foot as the mark of an unclean alliance.

But the story does not end until Jean also is brought within the drama of salvation. Xavier must go through further tribulation. Jean's thwarted love turns to bitter antipathy. A disillusioned curé adds yet another burden to his life. And a few minutes before his death he cries out from the midst of his own agony and dereliction " If only I had saved one single person." Yet it is because of that final sacrifice that Jean and Michele find their reconciliation and peace.

" Jean reached out a hand and turned on the light.

" ' Look at me, Michele,' he said. ' Let us look at one another. How can you bring yourself to speak of our present peace? Think what our life has become, every moment of it, now that he is not here.'

" She sat down on the bed. She sighed ' We are suffering but we are at peace. You know that that is true. He has given you his peace. Am I not right? '

" Jean hesitated, then said in a low voice ' Yes you are right. Yes, I am suffering as I have never suffered, yet, I am at peace, I, who never knew what peace meant, I, who, as a child, was thrashed by a brute, I, who, when I was sixteen, found out that the mother who I adored . . .'

" It was Michele who put the palm of her right hand over Jean's mouth. She said, ' What Xavier believed, you believe, too? '

" He did not deny it.

" ' Yes, Michele. I know now that love does exist in this world. But it is crucified in the world and we with it'. "

So we are brought back to Mauriac's central message— that whensoever and wheresoever the sufferings of Christ are reproduced in one of His servants, there salvation is being worked out: the salvation both of the sufferer and those for whom he is suffering. Christ's act is supreme, definitive, unapproachable. Yet it cannot be effective in the world to-day unless it is brought near through its re-enactment in the lives of saintly figures such as Xavier. There may, to be sure, be other ways—the whole sacramental system of the Church brings the merits of Christ to men—but Mauriac's concern is to portray the operations of the Divine Grace within the whole complex of inter-personal relationships. There it is the lamb who at all times bears the load of the sins of the world and through his passion heals and reconciles the lives of those whom he loves.

CHAPTER 3

THE ANGEL MUST HANG

HERMAN MELVILLE might well be called the John Bunyan of American literature. Coming out of a strong Puritan background, having little opportunity of formal education, living a life which was adventurous, often harassed, uneven, and in some ways tragic, each contrived to explore both the depths of human nature and the heights of supernature through prose whose excellence has seldom been surpassed in the history of the English language.

Melville was born in New York City in 1819. His father was of English Puritan descent, his mother of Dutch Calvinist, and he grew up within the framework of orthodox Presbyterianism. Because of the death of his father when he was only 13 and because of straitened family circumstances, Herman left school at an early age and after a period as a clerk in a bank, went to sea at the age of 18 and led the restless life of a seafarer for the next seven years. Then came a period of remarkable literary productivity culminating in the publication of *Moby Dick* in 1851. But by 1856 the bulk of his writing had been completed and in the next 30 years no major stories came from his pen.

At the very last, however, two years after his retirement

from his post as Inspector of Customs in New York, he began to work on another story. Progress was slow and he seems to have revised his manuscript again and again. When he died in 1891 many pages were still unfinished and it was not until 1924 that this final story, *Billy Budd*, was made available for general reading. And as, since that time, Melville's fame has grown, so the attempts to estimate the significance of this very small and very late work within his whole literary output have become more numerous. Is it just an interesting postscript not to be taken too seriously? Or is it a literary gem, a *Nunc Dimittis*, a gathering up of his total experience of life within one final testament of acceptance?

Apart from the question of its literary and dramatic merits or demerits, there has been an extraordinary divergence of opinion about its theological interpretation. Some would regard it as virtually neutral in its view of good and evil in the universe. The evil man perishes. So does the good. The struggle continues. Some would follow the radical view of Professor Lawrence Thompson who in his book *Melville's Quarrel with God*, regards Billy Budd as a final mockery of the Divine Ruler and a definite rejection of the universe which He made.

But the more generally accepted view (which I feel bound to accept myself) is that here, in abbreviated form, Melville is wrestling with the mighty forces which bring about the tragedies of human existence and is feeling after a way of reconciliation which he can accept with his mind as well as with his heart. He does not minimise the malignity of evil. He does not over-simplify the victory. He does not accept the Biblical witness to the Divine

46

reconciliation in any straightforward and obvious way. But it is impossible to overlook the delicate connections between his own symbolic language and that of the Bible and above all it is scarcely possible to follow the career of Billy Budd without being reminded of the career of Another, without, in short, recalling the main stages of the Passion Story which is our immediate concern.

Mr. W. H. Auden who, in his book *The Enchaféd Flood*, has a penetrating study of Billy Budd as a Christ-figure, has in an earlier poem given a convincing interpretation of the closing stages of Melville's life, showing the place that Billy occupies in the author's final understanding of the conflict between good and evil. He had discovered the simple truth that

> " *Evil is unspectacular and always human,*
> *And shares our bed and eats at our own table,*
> *And we are introduced to Goodness every day,*
> *Even in drawing-rooms among a crowd of faults;*
> *He has a name like Billy and is almost perfect,*
> *But wears a stammer like a decoration:*
> *And every time they meet the same thing has to happen;*
> *It is the Evil that is helpless like a lover*
> *And has to pick a quarrel and succeeds,*
> *And both are openly destroyed before our eyes* "

So now

> " *He stood upon the narrow balcony and listened:*
> *And all the stars above him sang as in his childhood*
> *' All, all is vanity,' but it was not the same;*
> *For now the words descended like the calm of mountains—*

47

—Nathaniel had been shy because his love was selfish—
But now he cried in exultation and surrender
' The Godhead is broken like bread. We are the pieces.' "

And sat down at his desk and wrote a story.

II

In a brief preface Melville quickly reveals his pre-
occupation with the conflict of opposites which is so
marked a feature of human existence. The French
Revolution he notes was motivated and impelled by the
urge to right hereditary wrongs; but straightway the
revolution itself became more oppressive than kings.
Similarly a revolution in the navy at Spithead was aimed
at real abuses and yet within a short time its continuation
at the Nore was merely wild and excessive. There is, in
other words, no simple defeat of wrong by right—
though Melville adds significantly that in each case the
final outcome of the revolution was a noticeable advance
in social ethics. Only through the (often violent) clash of
good and evil can society be reformed.

Having thus introduced his major theme Melville
proceeds to tell his story. As often before it is set in the
world of seafaring which he knew so well but it is no
longer the world of adventurous vessels in the South Seas
or of whaling expeditions from New Bedford but that of
the Royal Navy and King's Regulations. The hero is a
" Handsome Sailor," a youth of twenty-one named
Billy Budd who had been impressed into the King's Service

from the merchantman *Rights of Man* in which he had been serving. Making no demur at the change, he quickly adapted himself to fresh surroundings and soon won both the admiration and affection of his new comrades. The captain of the man-of-war was a certain Edward Fairfax Vere; commonly known as Starry Vere, exceptional by reason both of his literary tastes and of his moral earnestness, somewhat mysterious, somewhat withdrawn. The other chief character in the story is the master-at-arms, John Claggart, a man whose general appearance marks him out as of some distinction but whose behaviour is such as to suggest something sinister and even cruel in his make-up. These three are to be the chief actors in the drama.

Everything now revolves around one unexpected factor: Claggart's malign attitude towards Billy Budd. Small incidents begin to disturb Billy but at first he is frankly incredulous. Why could anyone have a grudge against him? Melville takes time to explore the mystery of irrational hatred before recounting a more serious incident in which a crafty attempt is made to involve his hero in a mutinous plot. It is not hard to see Claggart's hand in this new development but Billy still goes on in a kind of maze, conscious of his own complete innocence but gradually coming to the realisation that a network of inexplainable evil is closing in upon him.

At length the crisis comes. Carefully choosing his time, the master-at-arms appears before the captain, asking permission to inform him of a matter of some importance. Thereupon, cleverly playing upon the dangers of a revolutionary situation, he openly accuses Billy Budd of being a disloyal character who is only waiting for the opportunity to incite his shipmates to open rebellion. Captain Vere is not impressed. He orders that the young sailor shall be immediately summoned to his presence in order that he may have the opportunity of clearing himself of what the captain is convinced is a baseless charge.

A dramatic scene follows. Claggart repeats the accusation. Billy is literally dumbfounded. He tries to speak but his one obvious physical defect, a slight stammer, holds him tongue-tied. Though encouraged by Captain Vere to take his time, Billy is in an agony of desire to clear himself and suddenly, quick as the flame from a discharged cannon at night, his right arm shot out, and Claggart dropped to the deck, dead. For a moment all are stunned. Then comes the inevitable judgment. A drum-head court is convened, it struggles to find some way of escape for the prisoner but there is no redress. Billy must die, and that immediately. In the fleet a mortal punishment must not be delayed and the sentence will be carried out at the yard-arm in the early morning watch.

But Melville succeeds in painting three unforgettable scenes before describing the actual execution. One is the visit of Captain Vere to Billy Budd for the purpose of communicating the sentence to him: the second the public announcement by the captain to the ship's company of the offence and its consequent judgment; the third the visit of the chaplain to the condemned man. These, however, are only slight delays. The action moves swiftly to the early morning and the rising sun and the ascent of the tragic hero to his doom. A few significant details and the simple story ends. Melville's final commentary on the conflict between good and evil has been written and we are left to interpret the meaning as best we may.

III

Before touching on the theological implications of this dramatic story let us look at some of its significant features. Its setting is important. Here is an all-male company, travelling together within a strictly limited environment, cut off from the land and all that it implies. They have in one sense withdrawn from the natural, though in another sense they have a limited dominion over the natural. For as Melville says, the ocean, " is inviolate Nature primeval " and those who are on it are both cut off from the land which symbolises past tradition and poised precariously over the sea which symbolises present danger and uncertainty. There is no longer any direct contact with the home and the familiar community: there is the constant anxiety that primeval nature will once again swallow up its own. In such a situation law and discipline have a tremendously significant part to play. They crystallise in clear directives the lessons learned by former generations: they hold man constantly on the alert in the struggle with the forces that would otherwise overwhelm him. The situation may seem in some measure artificial and yet it is symbolic of the actual life of frontier-communities—and

51

not least that of the settlers of New England—wherever found.

In these situations the all-important time-dimension is the present moment (or to use modern terminology the existential " now "). Those in the ship must be ready for immediate action. Especially is this true in time of war or of threatened revolution. All time is, as it were, gathered up into one concentrated moment. All history can be effected by what happens in a single, critical event. Precedents are largely irrelevant. The law may give general guidance but even so a particular action is uniquely significant. In *Billy Budd* the short span of time covered by the story gathers all its intensity into a period of less than 24 hours within which the hero is accused, tested, condemned, executed. The sense of once-for-all-ness comes to the reader with immense power as he allows the story to make its impact upon him.

Within this simple space-time setting, the fullest scope is found for the delineation of the central characters and it is here that the fascination of the story is to be found. Captain Vere is a noble representative of the majesty of the law and the inviolability of reason. He comes of aristocratic stock but does not parade the fact. He had shown himself a gallant officer in action but does not trade on his physical prowess. His great strength derives from an inner reserve compounded of an inflexible determination to enforce discipline and of an unbending resolution to build upon well-established facts. He had, it is true, his moments of unearthly vision—his very nick-name " Starry " symbolised his ability to rise above the dull and the ordinary—but his vision, it may be guessed,

was focused more upon the exquisite orders and har-
monies of the created universe than upon the passions
and potentialities of redeeming love. He was, says
Melville, a man of settled convictions, honest, direct,
conscientious, completely dedicated to duty, cool-headed,
self-controlled: a well-nigh perfect embodiment, we may
add, of the Puritan ideal.

John Claggart is the very opposite. He is twisted,
tortuous, finally inexplicable. Even Melville despairs of
portraying him accurately and falls back upon the
concept of the " mystery of iniquity." It is not that
Claggart is dissolute, degraded or utterly repulsive. He
bears marks of good breeding, of more than average
intelligence, of a real distinction in facial appearance.
There are suspicions of some irregularity in his conduct
before he joined the navy but nothing is certain. And
once he had enlisted, his " superior capacity, consti-
tutional sobriety, ingratiating deference to superiors,
together with a peculiar ferreting genius manifested on a
singular occasion, all this capped by a certain austere
patriotism, abruptly advanced him to the position of
master-at-arms."

But although these are the surface impressions there is
always the sense of something underground, something
equivocal, something distorted, something subconscious
(Melville almost uses the term as he writes of the *depths* of
human nature), something utterly irrational in Claggart.
Melville is obviously fascinated by this mystery of
iniquity. In a passage of profound psychological insight
he isolates the passion of envy as probably the most
powerful force working in Claggart's heart. It is not

precisely the envy of Iago whose malignity was most stirred by the sight of virtue in others. In the case of Claggart it was the case of unsullied innocence that awoke in him a multiplicity of feelings—an intense desire to be identified with it, a cynical attitude of disdain towards it, a burning passion to annihilate it. Throughout the story it is the mixture of motives, the ambivalence of passions that is so hard to describe. Melville tries the symbolism of the ferret and the rat, of the beggars and rakers of the garbage, of Guy Fawkes prowling in underground chambers. But in the end there is no adequate symbolism, no final explanation. Such a nature is bound to act itself out and embrace its inevitable doom.

" With no power to annul the elemental evil in himself, though he could hide it readily enough; apprehending the good, but powerless to be it; what recourse is left to a nature like Claggart's, surcharged with energy as such natures almost invariably are, but to recoil upon itself, and, like the scorpion for which the Creator alone is responsible, act out to the end its allotted part? "

Between the captain and the master-at-arms stands the foretopman, the handsome sailor, Billy Budd. If it is hard to portray the mystery of subterranean iniquity, it is even harder to give a true picture of unfallen man, man in the foretop, man as the innocent child of God. Yet this is what Melville attempts to do through the figure of Billy Budd. There is something mysterious about his origin. He is obviously of noble descent but knows nothing of his parentage. His physical appearance leaves nothing to be desired: there is masculine strength and rustic beauty, a reposeful good-nature and a quick fellow-feeling, a joy in living and a freedom of movement all of which make him of heroic stature.

But his moral qualities are no less striking. He is intelligent but unspoiled by intellectual pride: he is upright but untouched by self-consciousness. The master of the *Rights of Man* cannot speak too highly of him. " My best man," " The jewel," " My peacemaker," " The flower of the flock." " It was black, I tell you, aboard the *Rights* here. But Billy came; and it was like a Catholic priest striking peace in an Irish shindy. Not that he preached to them or said or did anything in particular, but a virtue went out of him." " He is the nearest conceivable approach to that innocent nature which had in its simplicity never willed malice or experienced the reactionary bite of that serpent."

Only in two respects does Melville allow that his hero was subject to common human weaknesses. On the physical side there was no visible blemish but there was a strange vocal defect. Normally his voice was strong and musical and it was entirely natural for him to sing. But under sudden provocation or at a time of intense heart-feeling he was liable to hesitate, to stutter, even to be completely incapable of speech. This on the physical side. On the moral side the defect was exactly the opposite. Though utterly free from any kind of conscious attempt to win approval or popularity amongst his shipmates he yet found it extraordinarily difficult to say " No " to any proposal which was not obviously irrational or illegal. He was indeed slow to apprehend anything that was subtle and suggestive and with his love of free action he was liable to be involved in difficulties before he knew quite what was happening. On occasion too slow to speak, too quick to act—these were the only defects which Melville could discern in the general character of his hero. His was the innocence and trustfulness of the child: in him there was a spirit of purity and grace which looked out from his welkin eyes as from windows. " By his original constitution aided by the co-operating influences of his lot " Billy stood for what " Adam presumably might have been ere the urbane Serpent wriggled himself into his company."

IV

The plot, the setting and the characters are now before us. But it needs no special insight to see that there is a wider framework of reference to which, in indirect ways, the author is constantly pointing his readers. He himself had been brought up under the shadow of a great theological system and although it is quite evident that Melville was not prepared to accept all of its dogmas without question yet even when he was criticising or opposing he was still moving within the framework of its general assumption.

For the Calvinist the supreme reality was the God who had established the universe by His righteous decrees and whose laws were inviolable. Yet within this universe was the creature man who had rebelled against his Creator and had brought upon himself and his descendants the utter condemnation which his crime deserved. It was only by the infinite mercy of God that a way had been found to rescue a chosen company from perdition through the salvation wrought by the perfectly obedient Son. This chosen company—the elect—had been called out from the world of sin and damnation and while journeying to their heavenly destiny were being sanctified by the gracious working of the Divine Spirit.

That Melville could not accept this Calvinist orthodoxy as it stood is abundantly clear. It was too simple, too logical, too legalistic as a final interpretation of human existence. Yet he would not, like some—and especially like the transcendentalists of his day—abandon it altogether. He was too well aware of what Matthiessen calls " the titanic uncontrollable forces which seem to dwarf man altogether " to indulge in any facile humanism. He was altogether too conscious of the mystery of human depravity to reject out of hand the doctrine of original sin. How then can he construct a less rigid conception of the Divine Ruler, a more profound representation of human sin and a more realistic dramatisation of the act of redemption? Through *Billy Budd* he attempts, I believe, to achieve each of these aims and although it would obviously be absurd to look for a new system of theology in one short novel there are, I suggest, profound insights in this story which are worthy to be incorporated into any larger treatment of the doctrine of atonement.

In most respects Captain Vere represents the Puritan ideal. His allegiance is not to nature but to given law. His director is not the heart but the head. His concern is not with the intention but the act. His appeal is not to private conscience but to the imperial code. His responsibility is not primarily to the individual but to the whole society. His mien is grave, his attitude such as to command complete respect. As lord of the limited company on shipboard he symbolises in a very real way Him who is Lord of all mankind. And as such there is nothing at times to distinguish him from the man who in New England society was the accredited representative of the Divine will. When he gathered the sailors and briefly recounted to them the events leading up to the sentence of judgment on Billy: " Their captain's announcement was listened to by the throng of standing sailors in a dumbness like that of a seated congregation of believers in Hell listening to their clergyman's announcement of his Calvinistic text."

All this is true. Yet Melville contrives to show a very different side to the character of Captain Vere and thereby opens the door to a new understanding of the inner nature of God Himself. In the first place he stresses the fact that the law and the discipline which must necessarily be enforced are related to an essentially unnatural situation. It is because men are living in a state of potential or actual *war* that the sacredness of law must be upheld. Melville was sufficient of a realist to know that human life as we experience it is in very truth a conflict, a war between good and evil, a struggle between harmony and discord, between order and passion. It is because the human situation is as it is that the dominant manifestation of the Divine activity in the world is seen as the upholding of the law and the enforcing of its judgments.

But even more important is the fact that this is not the full revelation of the Divine that man can receive. Captain

Vere unhesitatingly acknowledges the legitimacy of the
pull of the Natural, he recognises the existence of what
he calls the feminine in man. Above all his general
attitude towards Billy is that of a father who believes
in him, understands his true quality and identifies
himself with him in the agony which he endures. Only
because of the wholly unnatural condition of the total
human situation must the law be allowed to take its
predestined course.

This inward compassion which is the deepest truth of
the Divine Being is expressed by hint and inference
rather than by open proclamation. But in one moving
passage, Melville takes his place with Bushnell and
McLeod Campbell and other nineteenth century prophets who in their reaction from a too logical orthodoxy
saw the momentary vision of the Cross in the heart of
God Himself. The scene is that in which Captain Vere
communicates the findings of the court to the prisoner.
It takes place in the secrecy of the stateroom and its
exact nature was never known. But in view of the
character of the two men, " each radically sharing in the
rarer qualities of one nature," Melville makes certain
conjectures. He imagines the full disclosure by Captain
Vere, including his own complete trust in Billy, responded
to by Billy with a sort of joy that he should so have been
regarded by his captain.

" Even more may have been. Captain Vere in the end
may have developed the passion sometimes latent under
an exterior stoical or indifferent. He was old enough
to have been Billy's father. The austere devotee of
military duty, letting himself melt back into what remains

primeval in our formalised humanity may in the end have caught Billy to his heart, even as Abraham may have caught Isaac on the brink of resolutely offering him up in obedience to exacting behest. But there is no telling the sacrament—seldom if in any case revealed to the gadding world—wherever, under circumstances at all akin to those here attempted to be set forth, two of great nature's nobler order embrace. There is privacy at the time, inviolable to the survivor, and holy oblivion, the sequel to diviner magnanimity, providentially covers all at last.

" The first to encounter Captain Vere in the act of leaving the compartment was the senior lieutenant. The face he beheld, for the moment one expressive of the agony of the strong, was to that officer, though a man of fifty, a startling revelation."

In such a passage, and particularly in such a phrase as " the agony of the strong," Melville bears witness to his own mature conception of the most inward character of God Himself.

In direct correspondence with his wider conception of the nature of God is Melville's deeper understanding of the complexity of human sin. Sin is the transgression of law—that is its most obvious form. As such it can be isolated, exposed, judged. A clear logic and a resolute will can deal with sin when it is nothing more than this. But Melville knew too much about the distortions and irrationalities within human relationships even amongst the saints of New England to allow him to remain satisfied with any view of sin which confined it to open rebellion against given law. It was far more subtle,

mysterious, inexplicable. And in the drama of the relationship between Claggart and Billy Budd, Melville
tries to probe more deeply into what in the end must still
remain the " mystery of iniquity."

Not that this was the first time that Melville had
assayed the task. Amidst the storm and fury of *Moby
Dick* we see a man of heroic stature vainly trying to hunt
down the demoniac incarnation of evil in order to destroy
it. Ruthless, relentless, pitiless in his quest, he becomes
a fiend himself—and the struggle never ends. But in
Billy Budd the setting is quieter, the action more re-
strained, though the penetration may be even more
profound. Indeed Mr. E. M. Forster commenting on
the fact that so often evil is but feebly envisaged in
fiction, claims that it is in *Billy Budd* that we can begin to
see how evil really works.

" Evil to most novelists " he writes, " is either sexual
or social, or something very vague for which a special
style with implications of poetry is thought suitable.
They want it to exist in order that it may kindly help
them with the plot and evil not being kind, generally
hampers them with a villain—a Lovelace or Uriah Heep
—who does more harm to the author than to the fellow
characters. For a real villain we must turn to a story of
Melville's called *Billy Budd*."*

He goes on to point out how evil is " labelled and
personified instead of slipping over the ocean and round
the world " and how in Melville's conception it reaches
straight back into the universal without being cramped
and restricted by detailed questions of the individual

* E. M. Forster *Aspects of the Novel*. 181-2.

conscience. In the key-passage of his analysis of depravity Melville draws on Plato as well as on the Hebrew prophets. Call it original sin or natural depravity, here is this strange aberration in man which " folds itself in the mantle of respectability. It has its certain negative virtues serving as silent auxiliaries. It is not going too far to say that it is without vices or small sins. There is a phenomenal pride in it that excludes them from anything —never mercenary or avaricious. In short, the depravity here meant partakes nothing of the sordid or sensual. It is serious but free from acerbity. Though no flatterer of mankind, it never speaks ill of it.

" But the thing which in eminent instances signalises so exceptional a nature is this: though the man's even temper and discreet bearing would seem to intimate a mind peculiarly subject to the law of reason, not the less in his soul's recesses he would seem to act in complete exemption from that law having apparently little to do with reason further than to employ it as an ambidexter implement for effecting the irrational. That is to say: toward the accomplishment of an aim which in wantonness of malignity would seem to partake of the insane, he will direct a cool judgment sagacious and sound."

Though rejecting, then, the rigid definitions of inherited guilt and total depravity Melville was by no means prepared to entertain a sunny view of human nature. There was, he judged, such a thing as an evil nature which could combine cleverness and malignity in a terrible way. It was fanatically opposed to the innocent and the beautiful and would stop at nothing in order to encompass its downfall. In Claggart we see " a depravity according to nature," mysterious but deadly in its malignity and malevolence. And when his corpse was being raised " it was like handling a dead snake."

V

There is a saying of Calvin's which expresses a fundamental principle of his developed theological system, " If the Son of God had not been free from all sin, we should have had no right to look for expiation from his death."

In other words, only an innocent victim, in the Calvinist view, could take the place of the guilty and die in their stead. Only a sinless offering could make due satisfaction to God's righteous judgment on human sin. Though not necessarily accepting this principle in its dogmatic form, Melville was not likely to abandon it altogether. How could he portray innocence, sinlessness, the untainted expression in humanity of goodness and beauty and truth? How could he depict an offering which would not only satisfy the outward demands of the law but would still more express the spirit of complete reconciliation between man and God? Through the character and the final willing surrender of Billy Budd, Melville makes his supreme attempt to give an aesthetic representation of the Christ-figure and of His perfect self-offering on behalf of mankind.

Yet at first sight Billy is far more akin to the unconscious Adam than to the conscious Christ. In his important book *The American Adam*, Professor R. W. B. Lewis puts forward the hypothesis that the force which has shaped American literature over the past century and a half, more than any other, has been the Adamic myth—the idea, that is, that the American is a new Adam of heroic stature delivered from sinister influences of the past by the very fact of his new environment on the western side of the Atlantic, and destined to advance into a future bright with the promise of bodily prosperity and spiritual well-being. Though at first this hope was held in check, at least on its physical side, by the stern tradition of Calvinism which concentrated attention upon the spiritual joys reserved for God's elect, the gradual emergence of a secular Utopianism meant that the new Adam could, in the view of many, go forward to his full development without need to overcome the *damnosa hereditas* of original sin and without serious hindrance from the evil world around him.

Melville had little sympathy with this sunny optimism but he was prepared to accept the symbolism of an Adam-figure passing from the bliss of innocence to his full stature as the Christ-figure, in and through the encounter with falsehood and wrong. The transition, however, does not take place in any obvious way. The handsome sailor of the first part of the narrative, the welkin-eyed Baby Budd living peacefully in the *Rights of Man*, bears many of the marks of Adam: the lamb-like hero of the second part, the agonising standard-bearer of the truth in the conflict with envy and malignity, bears many of the marks of the Christ. Somehow the change-over is made. Does it happen off-stage as Mr. Auden suggests, in the final interview between Billy and Captain Vere? Or does it

64

happen in that moment when the hitherto almost passive character of the genial foretopman strikes fire in a consuming lightning flash as he joins issues with evil incarnate? Or does it even come to pass, as Professor Lewis infers, more within the consciousness of the reader than in the character of the hero? Innocence and love, already present in Adam, are seen to be indestructible and impelling only in the context of the saving work of Christ.

However we seek to interpret the way by which the Christ-figure emerges, there can be little doubt that from the moment when Billy's right arm shoots out and Claggart drops to the deck, the theme of the sacrifice of the innocent victim becomes explicit. In one sense, of course, Billy was not innocent. His action under severe provocation had resulted in the death of a fellow-man. Yet in another sense he was guiltless, for his action had been that of a champion attacking evil in its most concentrated form. The central paradox of redemption appears: the champion who destroys sin must himself be destroyed that a full expiation may be made and a new order of life established.

There is no need to enlarge on the way in which Melville deals with this paradox. In the character of Captain Vere, love and law, the father and the military disciplinarian, are in constant tension. " It is the divine judgment of Ananias! " Yet the instrument of this judgment must himself be condemned. " Struck dead by an Angel of God. Yet the Angel must hang! " Billy, he knows, is true to the King. Yet his deed deserves nothing less than the final penalty. In the last interview Captain Vere may have

65

caught Billy to his heart. Yet a short time afterwards he was speaking to the ship's company in clear terms and concise about the execution which was to take place in the early morning watch. And in the lengthy admonition to the members of the court-martial the whole stress lies upon the duty of judge and jury alike not to allow private feelings of compassion, even the private conscience to deflect them from the dread responsibility of adhering to and administering the imperial law under which they all serve. The pure in heart who seeks to act in a sinful world which is held in check by the Divine law inevitably brings down the final penalty upon his own head—though Captain Vere's own dying words give a clear indication that only through such a death can man's salvation be found.

Billy's own conduct in the last scenes is of a quality that cannot fail to remind us of the Passion Story of the Gospels. He speaks little but his few words recall the answers of the Christ to Pilate. When the sentence has been pronounced and he is waiting for his death he is seen to be lying on deck surrounded by guns and carriages all painted black, himself, clad in the white jumper and white duck trousers belonging to his rank, with " the look of a slumbering child in the cradle," touched from time to time by the happy light born of some wandering reminiscence or dream! He was utterly without fear as the ship's chaplain was to find when he came to prepare him for death. There is no recrimination, no resentment. He is led as a lamb to the slaughter: he commits himself without flinching to the perfect righteousness of God.

The execution scene in Chapter 22 is deeply moving. The light symbolism is again prominent. The Calvinistic note of ascribing all glory to God the Father even when the agony of the Son " alone must have been in their hearts, even as he was in their eyes " rings out confidently. And the references to the Saviour of all mankind is unmistakable in the oft quoted paragraph: " The hill, deliberately recovering from the periodic roll to leeward, was just regaining an even keel, when the last signal, the preconcerted dumb one, was given. At the same moment it chanced that the vapoury fleece hanging low in the east was shot through with a soft glory as of the fleece of the Lamb of God seen in a mystical vision and simultaneously therewith, watched by the wedged mass of upturned faces, Billy ascended; and ascending, took the full rose of the dawn."

It only remains to add that with the coming of the full day, " the circumambient air in the cleanness of its serenity was like smooth white marble in the polished block not yet removed from the marble-dealers yard."

In a note to his manuscript Melville was to add, " Here ends a story not unwarranted by what sometimes happens in this incomprehensible world of ours—Innocence and infamy, spiritual depravity and fair repute." In other words, there is no possibility of a completely satisfying intellectual solution to the problem of evil nor is there any prospect of a final triumph of right over wrong in the conditions of the present world-order. But the sacrifice of the Son of God, remembered in every age, can inspire men to suffer and even to die in the faith that it is the

Lamb of God, the innocent, the true, the pure, who bears away the sin of the world. As Professor Mathiessen has so beautifully said, " After all he had suffered Melville could endure to the end in the belief that though good goes to defeat and death, its radiance can redeem life." (*American Renaissance*.)

CHAPTER 4

THE SHEPHERD IS SMITTEN

THE TRADITION of Eastern Christendom has become known to the West chiefly through the writings of Russian drama- tists and novelists. And of these none has made a deeper impression than Dostoievsky with his extraordinary insight into the structure of human relationships and his profound understanding of the place of religion in the whole range of human existence.

The figure of the Christ fascinated Dostoievsky. The sayings and experiences recorded in the Gospels were constantly in his mind and it is quite obvious that more than one of the characters in his novels is meant to be a Christ-figure, an imaginary incarnation within a later historical situation of the Divine Humanity revealed in the Christ of Galilee. Alyosha pre-eminently but also Sonia and Prince Myshkin and the central figure of the legend of the Grand Inquisitor—these are all in their own ways reproductions or representations of the Christ. Yet so far as I am aware Dostoievsky does not set out to give a precise reproduction of the Passion Story in any of his novels. There is no attempt to portray one of his Christ-figures passing through the stages of vocation, testing, opposition, rejection, suffering, no direct parallel to the Gospel record of Christ Himself.

For an Eastern writer's reproduction of the Passion Story, therefore, I turn to a more modern novelist, a Greek, rather than a Russian, Nikos Kazantzakis, who was born in Crete in 1883 and died only in 1957. He was a man of unusual breadth of culture. He studied law at Athens, philosophy in Paris, literature and art in Germany and Italy. But his writing was in his own language and included poems, plays, novels and philosophy. His name was proposed for the Nobel Prize but the award was not actually made.

So far very few of his works have been translated into English. A few poems, two novels, *Zorba the Greek* and *Freedom and Death*, and most recently a remarkable epic *The Odyssey: A Modern Sequel*, have revealed something of the power and imagination of his writing. But for our own purpose the altogether significant book is the novel which, in 1954, appeared in America under the title *The Greek Passion* and in England as *Christ Recrucified*. Hailed by competent critics as a work of high artistic excellence, the novel does not seem to have made any deep impression in the West though interest in it has been revived through the production of a film, *He Who Must Die*, based upon its story. The film made in Crete under the direction of Jules Dassin is one of the most moving religious productions of modern times. The clash of the two Greek Popes, one leading the band of starving but inspired peasants, the other keeping guard over his well-fed but spiritually impoverished village, is superbly portrayed within a setting perfectly adapted to the story.

Thomas Mann has written of the " poetic tact " which Kazantzakis reveals in his handling of the Passion Story.

This judgment is well-merited for whereas Kazantzakis introduces the story in the most natural way possible its actual working out in the contemporary situation is exciting and dramatic, often surprising and sometimes even repellent to the Western imagination. Through the novel we can look at the Passion and Death and Resurrection through Eastern eyes and learn theology through a noble creation of the poetic imagination. What then are the essential elements of the novelist's own story?

II

It is Easter Tuesday in a prosperous Greek village. Though the inhabitants tend to chafe under the yoke of the Turkish dominion, life is comfortable and pleasant enough in most respects. They are content to accept the counsel of their Pope which is to pay the necessary taxes in kind, to give proper respect to the Turkish Agha and to live peaceably with one another enjoying the fruits of the land. On this day, however, something unusual is happening: the villagers are being summoned to the little church to learn who are to play the leading parts in the Passion Play (an event which happens every seven years) which will be performed at the following Easter season.

So we are introduced to the varied assemblage of village characters. There is the Pope himself, passionate and sensual and yet in his own way a prophet. There are the five elders of the village-council, a mixed group, vivacious, rascally, often humorous and withal possessed of certain rough virtues. These are the simple characters on whom the choice falls to play the leading parts— Manolios the shepherd who is to be the Christ: Michelis his friend who will be John: Kostandis the café-keeper as James, Kannakos the carrier as Peter, two of the elders as Pilate and Caiaphas and finally the red-haired ruffian of the village as Judas and his paramour, the widow Katerina, as Mary Magdalen. The selection is made with immense zest and rude humour and the stage is set for the enactment of the Passion, not so much in the Mystery of the following year as in the actual events of the coming months.

For Manolios has scarcely had chance to consider with his intimate friends the nature of their calling when their own life and that of the whole village is disrupted by the arrival of a marching horde of starving peasants, survivors of a Turkish massacre. Led by their Pope Fotis they ask only for land, land where they can find a hold and again take root. They have brought the bones of their fathers with them to become the foundation of a new village. But the Pope of Lycovrissi, Pope Grigoris, will have none of it. Seeking an excuse to drive the refugees into the hills he is suddenly presented with one ready made when a poor woman collapses screaming. He only needs to utter the dreaded word ' cholera ' for it to become evident to all that the starving band must go. So the pathetic marchers withdraw to the mountain, determined to build their own Jerusalem even amongst the rocks and stones and to trust in the mercy of the prophet Elijah, the patron of the mountain, who loves the persecuted.

The two rival camps are now established. In Lyco-vrissi, Pope Grigoris and his elders seek at all costs to preserve peace with the Turk, full larders for themselves, and the regular cycle of marriage and song in the community. In the mountain Pope Fotis and his followers hold on in hope, dig the foundations of a new village but see their plight growing steadily worse. The chosen Christ-band begin to accept the consequences of their vocation by attempting to smuggle relief to those in need but trouble is soon brewing. Pope Grigoris and his supporters will not allow themselves to be easily despoiled of their possessions and the drama begins to unfold.

There is in fact a double cycle. First within Lycovrissi itself, there are jealousies and intrigues and violent passions: the Turkish Agha and his beloved male-attendant who is mysteriously killed, the Judas-figure and the prostitute Katerina who deserts him, Manolios and his betrothed who renounces him. Finally Manolios gives himself up as a sacrifice on behalf of the village threatened with destruction by the outraged Agha and is only saved at the last moment by the intervention first of Katerina who receives the knife into her own bosom, and then of the Agha's house-keeper who exposes the real culprit. Manolios has taken upon himself the burden of his own people and has borne shame and the pangs of death in their stead. But there is a second passion yet to come.

The second cycle, gathering impetus after Katerina's death, reveals Manolios and his friends taking upon themselves the burden of the people of the mountain and doing all in their power to save them from extinction. On the day of St. Elijah, when the harvest is in, Manolios raises the standard. He has taken on new stature as the representative of Christ and now dares to summon his fellow villagers to share their food with the refugees. At first they are moved to compassion and begin to make promises of aid. But Pope Grigoris is furious. He accuses Manolios of fomenting revolution and finally the council of elders banishes him from the village. " Get out " cries the Pope, " with the curse of God." " The curse of the notables and popes" Manolios replies, " it is you, the popes, who crucified Christ. If he came down upon earth again, you would crucify him afresh, Goodbye."

So the struggle to the death is joined. Manolios throws in his lot with Pope Fotis and the people of the mountain. First they come down peaceably, led by Pope Fotis and Manolios, to seek a share in the vintage celebrations. Grigoris however is determined to give away nothing and even calls upon the Agha to lead a charge of his troops to scatter them. Their position worsens until with the coming of winter they are desperate. Manolios and his friends see no other way to help them than by stealing from the well-stocked village stores, but even this is only a palliative. There is only one final possibility: it is war. No longer does Manolios represent the Christ of mercy. He is setting free the face of the Christ of judgment. But when the fight is at last joined it is Manolios who is captured and brutally killed in the little church by the hand of the man who had accepted the destiny of Judas, acting with the blessing of the Pope who claimed to be the representative of God Himself. And the story ends with Pope Fotis muttering "In vain, my Christ, in vain: two

thousand years have gone by and men crucify you still."
And then " In the name of Christ " he cried, " the march
begins again; courage, my children." And again they
resumed their interminable march towards the East.

III

The setting of this fascinating drama is intimately
related to the drama itself. The small-scale community
with its roots deep in the limited parcel of land on which
it dwells, and forming with that particular area a single
living organism—this has always been the typical and the
ideal form of existence in Greece. From the days of the
old city-state down to the modern small town or large
village, the pattern has been roughly the same. The
compact yet varied community, living under the direction
of its elders, surrounded by the fields and the flocks and
vineyards on which it depends for the necessities of life,
only disturbed by the fierce, unnatural, foreigner, the
Turks whom it must pacify and perhaps in due course
expel.

The community lives very close to the land. It shares
the seasonal variations, the moods, the success and failure
of the good earth itself. " It was Easter Tuesday.
Exquisite weather, tender; spring sun and rain; the
lemon blossoms were fragrant, the trees budding, the
grass reviving, Christ rising from every clod. The
Christians were coming and going across the square and
embracing one another with the Paschal greeting,
" Christ is risen! Risen indeed! "—after which they

75

would go and sit at Kostandis's café or in the middle of the square under the old plane-tree. They ordered narghiles and coffee and at once there began an endless chatter, like the light rain.

"This is what it'll be like in Paradise," hazarded Charalambes the beadle, "soft sunshine, a gentle rain falling without a sound, lemon-trees in blossom, narghiles and agreeable conversation, for ever and ever."

Life on this earth is at its best an earnest of life in Paradise. But not in any abstract or purely spiritual sense. A full life here is intimately related to the natural order—to the plane-tree and the falling rain and the delicious lemon blossoms and the taste of coffee and the springing grass. Man must live with the earth, wait with it, die with it, rise again with it. There is no separation between the natural and the spiritual, between the temporal and the eternal. All belong to the one living Divine organism which is indestructible.

On the other hand to be deprived of a piece of land to call one's own—this is the supreme disaster. All the refugees asked was land, land in which to put forth roots. "We have heard tell that you have waste land, for which you have no use: give it us, we will share it out, we will sow it, we will harvest it, we will make bread for all these starving people to eat. That's what we ask, Father."

And because no one would give land in the village of Lycovrissi, they determined to take possession of the mountain. "My children," cried Pope Fotis, "it is here, on this sheer mountain that, with God's aid, we shall take root. Man is like a tree; he needs earth. This is where we will put forth roots. I saw in a dream last night St.

George, our patron, riding on a white horse and behind him on its back the beautiful princess whom St. George had saved from the horrible monsters of the fountain; she was holding out towards him a ewer of gold and pouring out for him to drink—Who is this beautiful princess, my children? It is the soul of Greece, our soul! St. George has taken us up on his horse and has brought us here, on to this deserted mountain where we are. Last night I saw him in my dream; he stretched out his arm and placed in my hand the seed of a village—a little, little village in my palm, with its church, its school, its houses, its gardens—and he said to me: ' Plant it.' "

Nothing could more aptly describe the Greek ideal. The balanced community, planted in its own plot, nurtured by the gifts of nature, sensitive to nature's moods and changes, living and dying with the natural cycle, indestructible, free. And the Christ rises from every clod. Every clod of earth is also a Holy Sepulchre.

Even more significant, perhaps, is the attitude to time which emerges so clearly in the course of the narrative. As has so often been pointed out, time and history in the Greek view are not critical and particular but recurring and general. The cycle of events which make up Kazantzakis's story could have happened at any time in Greek history. The Turk happens to be the foreign overlord, but it might have been any other. The constant cry of faith rings out that Greece is immortal. She dies only to rise again. History literally repeats itself: the struggle between the affluent and the dispossessed, between the humble and the self-righteous, between the Christ and the Anti-Christ will never be brought to a

77

conclusion one way or the other. Every Eastertide Christ dies and rises again. In every conflict of good with evil He dies and rises again. In the revolving seasons He dies and rises again.

Michelis has just bidden farewell to the girl he loves and is wandering about the mountain while from below the songs of the vintage rise up to meet him.

" Michelis stopped; his heart was heavy with an insurmountable sadness; no, to him those were not vintage songs but funeral lamentations.

" Standing there, without stirring, he felt life turning on and on, inexorably, never stopping. The wheel of the earth was turning. It had now reached the vintage . . . The turn of the olives would come; then that of the birth of Christ . . . the almond trees would blossom afresh, the corn would be sown again, the harvest would come round. . . . It all went on as if Michelis were tied to that wheel and rose and fell with it under the sun, under the rain. Tied to it with him, day and night also rose and fell. Christ newborn, with them, grew, became a man, went forth resolutely to spread the word of God, was crucified, rose again, came down again from heaven the next year, was again crucified . . .

" Michelis, with his temples humming, felt his head seized by giddiness. He clung to a rock as though to stop the wheel, prevent it from turning. He slid to the ground and suddenly, for no apparent reason, burst into tears."

In other ways too, we are made aware of the never-ending cycle. The Passion Play takes place every seventh year thus becoming a seventh day of the new creation. The story itself moves in perfect harmony with the seasons

—the freshness and hope of springtime, the heat and passion of summer, the bounty and yet the foreboding of autumn, the rigour and even the cruelty of winter—all the prelude to another cycle and the repetition of the same pattern of events. Birth and Death, Spring and Autumn, Planting and Reaping, Joy and Suffering—all are included within the perpetual death and resurrection of the Christ Himself.

This symbolism of time moreover, is but one example of the wider symbolism which is characteristic of the Eastern outlook and comes to expression again and again in the story. There is for instance, the intensely moving description of the foundation of the new city on the barren mountain. How can a starved and ragged horde build a city? Yet they have the bones of their fathers, the tools of their labour and the seed of man. The bones of the fathers are set in the foundation and their potency is increased when the old man who had borne them on the march lies down and dies, his sacrificial blood bringing fertility to the new enterprise.

The boundaries are marked out with holy water, the gates are dedicated to Christ, the protector of the oppressed, to the Virgin, the comforter of the sorrowful, to St. George, the faithful shepherd and heroic labourer, to the last Byzantine King, the pledge of the restoration of Constantinople. All through the story the mountain is the place of austerity but also of purity, of human despair but also of divine hopefulness. It is for ever sanctified by the prophet Elijah and his chariot of fire which is none other than the sun riding in the glory of his strength. Liberty, heroism, sacrifice belong to the mountain.

" ' How ought we to love God, Father? ' Manolios asked one day.

' By loving men, my son.'

' And how ought we to love men? '

' By trying to guide them along the right path.'

' And what is the right path? '

' The one that rises.' "

The rising path is one of the key symbols of the whole book.

IV

The wider theological setting of the book is vividly expressed in one of the chapter titles: " God is a Potter. He works in mud." The phrase is Pope Fotis's and he is indeed the theologian amongst all the varied characters. His theology has grown out of his own life-experience, an experience in which he has seen the judgment and the mercy of God dramatically intertwined. He himself has been guilty of the most violent outbreaks of human passion which have parted him from God; yet through bitter loss and grief he has been brought back to him and now can praise God for all the evil and all the good which he has received.

First and foremost God is beyond all human understanding. Man is a blind earthworm at God's feet. What can he understand of incommensurable greatness? To illustrate his point Pope Fotis recounts the parable which he had learned from his superior in the monastery about a group of blind villagers desiring to gain some comprehension of the mighty elephant. Each touches some portion of its anatomy and gives his report. But how little the several reports reveal of the true nature of the animal. So on an infinitely larger scale it is with man's knowledge of God. He can recognise parts of his ways: but the thunder of his power who can understand?

The incident which leads Pope Fotis to embark on his most extended discourse is the appearance of the covering of repulsive flesh on Manolios's face. This has, in fact, been his salvation. For when he might have succumbed to the passionate urge of the flesh the leprous mask on his face had removed him far from any woman's interest.

Who, then, had brought about the mysterious and foul affliction?

" It's no demon, Manolios, that has settled on you. It is God who has clapped this mask upon you to save you. You were going towards the abyss, Manolios, you were on the edge of the gulf, and God fixed this flesh upon your face to make you stop."

" The three friends bent their heads, transfixed with terror. Shuddering, they felt that God besieges each one of us, like a lion. Sometimes you feel his breath, hear his roaring, see his eyes piercing the darkness.

" The pope seemed to guess their thoughts.

" ' My children ' he said, ' an eye is open in us day and night and watches. An ear is open deep in our heart and listens: God.'

" And Michelis cried: ' How can God let us live on the earth? Why doesn't he kill us to purify creation? '

" ' Because Michelis,' the pope answered, ' God is a potter; he works in mud. God is never in a hurry. He is still. He sees the future as though it were already past. He works in eternity. Let God work in silence, as he likes to do.' "

This is the authentic witness of Eastern Christendom. God is mysterious. The world is mysterious. The soul of man is mysterious. But faith is convinced that through all the mystery a wonderful process is being carried forward. Even in the smallest pebble, even in the humblest animal, even in the darkest soul, God is present fully. He does not despise the mud of earthy passions and sensuous desires. He does not wipe out the cruel, jealous, lustful sons of men. He watches and waits. He works in silence. And all the time the process of salvation continues and the shining vessels of His good pleasure are moulded to His design.

There is certainly no attempt on Kazantzakis's part to whitewash the human situation. The coarseness and sensuality and haughtiness of the Agha: the greed and cowardice and mercilessness of Michelis's father: the cunning and brutality and hypocrisy of Pope Grigoris— these are characteristic of three of the leading figures of the community. To see the four village heads in the prison awaiting almost certain execution is to see human nature at its most selfish and mean and pitiable. Yet even in the most depraved, salvation is constantly at work. " Haven't you seen, my brethren, how the caterpillar in winter enters and hides within a tightly shut shroud? Its head is transformed, it becomes fierce, it waits motionless. Slowly, in its vitals, in the midst of darkness, as labouring deliverance. Behind all that ugliness she is wearing a light down, a brilliant eye, wings. One fine spring

morning she pierces the shroud and comes out, a butterfly.
That is how, in us, through the darkness, deliverance is
busy."

How it comes about that out of one dark cavern a
butterfly emerges while in another a bed of festering evil
is created, remains a mystery. God is working in mud.
He gives to the world a Manolios, a Fotis, a Katerina.
But in the background we see a Grigoris, a Panayotaros,
an Agha and we know that Christ is still crucified in the
world. The struggle between good and evil never ceases.
But the resurrection of the Christ is the unshakable
promise of victory and the new creation.

v

To re-present the Passion of Christ through literature
and the drama is more natural to artists of the Orthodox
tradition than to writers of any other section of Christendom. The Passion, the Orthodox believes, is constantly
being re-enacted in the natural world, in the world of
human relationships, in the drama of the Eucharist, in
the mysteries of sacrament and passion-play. Kazantzakis makes little direct reference to the Eucharist but
weaves the passion-motif into every other aspect of the life
of the village. Nature dies and rises again. Manolios in
the first cycle dies in his complete surrender and sacrifice
and rises again in the Christ who still marches on.

As in Dostoievsky's re-presentation of the Christ-figure
much is made of the temptations which assail the Divine
Hero. In a very real sense, the temptation *is* the passion.

In the forefront stands the temptation of the flesh. Manolios is betrothed to Lenio and the urge is strong to consummate the marriage. But he knows that his acceptance of the Christ-vocation means that the wedding must be postponed at least until the end of the year. Hardly has this decision been communicated to the angry father, however, when a far more powerful temptation assails him. The widow Katerina has cast her eyes upon him and is prepared to use all her wiles to entrap him. From the chance encounter at the side of the fountain Manolios escapes unscathed but the image of the widow now haunts his imagination. On the one side he is aware of a genuine compassion which longs to help this woman who has sold herself to men. But on the other side there is a burning desire to accept what she is only too ready to offer.

" I left her but I took her with me, in my thoughts, in my blood, day and night I now dreamed only of her. I pretended to be thinking of Christ; lies! lies! It was of her I was thinking.

" One evening I could hold out no longer; I took the path—I was going to the widow. I told myself ' I'm going to save her soul. I'm going to talk to her and lead her into the way of God.' Lies! Lies! I was rushing to sleep with her. Then . . ."

Manolios's deliverance from this temptation is, perhaps, one of the less impressive parts of Kazantzakis's story. It comes about through the sudden eruption of the skin of his face in a kind of repulsive leprosy. So horrible is it that no woman would look at him. Until his soul is finally purged the loathsome mask remains. But when he is ready to be sacrificed, willingly, joyfully,

then to his amazement he finds that the mask is falling
from his face and that his skin is smooth again. The fire
of the temptation which has purged him of his pride and
his lust has made him a lamb ready to be led to the
slaughter on behalf of his fellow-villagers.

The account of the first crisis in which Manolios offers
himself to the fury of the Agha contains a strange mixture
of parallels and contrasts to the Passion Story of the
Gospels. The patience, innocence, strength and nobility
of the victim are not unworthy to be compared to the
virtues of the Christ. On the other hand, the sustained
lie by which Manolios takes upon himself the blame for
the murder of the boy Youssoufaki is unthinkable in the
Gospel context. The widow's sacrifice on Manolios's
behalf, the devotion of his followers who already have a
measure of faith:—

" It's for us he's dying, to save the village. Don't you
understand? He's taking on him the sins of us all, like
Christ "—these have no direct parallel in the original
narrative. But Katerina's motive is the same as that of
Mary Magdalen and the behaviour of the three followers
is obviously motivated by what they already know of the
salvation wrought by Christ Himself. But the final
result of what they do not hesitate to call Manolios's
" resurrection " is to bind them to him more closely than
ever before. Now in a real sense they have become his
body on earth. They are prepared to follow him wherever
he goes, to share his spirit of sacrifice, to leave everything
in the service of Christ. Henceforward the way for them
all leads to the mountain and they will walk together on
the rising path.

The second cycle of the Passion raises acute problems for those who have always lived within the Western tradition. The nature of the relationship between church and government, the view of revolution and bloodshed, the theories of society and property do not immediately commend themselves, and the question arises whether Manolios's ultimate death ought to be regarded as that of a Christ-figure or whether it is not rather the inevitable penalty of social revolution. There is in fact little in the Gospels to suggest that the death of Christ was brought about as a result of any startling innovations which he proposed concerning the ownership of property or the distribution of goods. He was crucified primarily because of his criticism of the religious authorities and because of his identification with the Messianic vocation. Yet in he story Manolios takes upon himself the burden of the starving followers of Pope Fotis and proposes a definite programme of social revolution to his own compatriots of Lycovrissi. It is this which arouses the implacable hatred of Pope Grigoris and the village elders and leads finally to his death.

But these are not the only difficulties. In the struggle which ensues Manolios and his followers and Pope Fotis use the weapons of war in the name of Christ. They are prepared to plunder old Ladas's house for the sake of the starving brethren and to take up arms in what they call a holy war.

"No one can go up to heaven" cries Pope Fotis, "unless he has first been victorious upon earth, and no one can be victorious upon earth if he does not struggle against it with fire, with patience, without resting. Man has only earth for his springboard if he would fly to heaven. All the Pope Grigorises, the Ladases, the Aghas, the big proprietors, are the forces of evil which it has been allotted us to combat. If we throw down our arms, we're lost here below on earth and up there in the sky! To suffer, undergo injustices and struggle without giving ground—that's what it means to be a *man*." And the inference is that it is only the man who is prepared to sacrifice himself in the struggle for liberty and justice who is acceptable to God.

So the final section of the book is devoted to the dramatic struggle between what Fotis calls bishops, popes and notables on the one side and two or three beggars with Christ in front on the other. For Christ, he says, is not always the kindly, easy, pacific figure. He is also a resolute warrior, the leader of the disinherited of the earth. Nothing can be done without blood being shed. And one day, Yannakos cries out " If Christ came down on earth to-day, on an earth like this one, what do you think He'd have on his shoulders? A cross? No, a can of petrol."

On the 22nd of December, the birthday of the prophet Elijah, the villagers from the mountain, armed and bearing slings, led by a standard-bearer displaying " the savage face of Christ," descend to the plain. Their orders are not to strike unless they are attacked. Their only concern is to take possession of gardens, vineyards, fields which are theirs by right and to labour in them that they may live. But the Lycovrissiots mobilise and march out behind Pope Grigoris to resist them to the death. There is a semi-humorous combat between the two

Popes, the champions of the two villages, which results in the humiliation and still more bitter fury of Pope Grigoris. But gradually everything converges upon Manolios. Nothing will satisfy Grigoris and his followers save the death of this arch-bolshevik, Manolios the excommunicated.

The last chapter reproduces many features of the Gospel-story, of the arrest and trial and death of Jesus. The Agha is persuaded to give the order for the arrest of Manolios and Panayotaros, the Judas-figure, is his tool. But there is no need to use force. Manolios gives himself up willingly and accepts the full responsibility for all that has happened. The crowd howls for his death and at length he is handed over to the will of Grigoris and his followers. Ironically the death scene is enacted before the altar of the village church. The crowd gathers within, the doors are locked and while Fotis and his followers are battering outside, Panayotaros plunges the dagger into Manolios's bosom. Pope Grigoris bends down, fills the hollow of his hand with blood and sprinkles the crowd, crying as he does so " May his blood fall upon the heads of us all." Yet in the very next breath he is giving the order to open the door and wash the stones quickly for " to-night, at midnight, we are celebrating the birth of Christ."

It is left to Pope Fotis to give the final commentary: " ' Dear Manolios,' he murmurs, ' you'll have given your life in vain; they killed you for having taken our sins upon you. . . . In vain, Manolios, in vain will you have sacrificed yourself.'

" He listened to the bell pealing gaily announcing that

Christ was coming down on earth to save the world. . . .
He shook his head and heaved a sigh; In vain, my Christ,
in vain, two thousand years have gone by and men crucify
You still. When will you be born, my Christ, and not be
crucified any more, but live among us for eternity? "

" Christ is in agony until the end of the world." This is
the famous word of an early Greek Father which reveals
the characteristic outlook of Eastern Christendom. The
Incarnation is no afterthought designed simply to deal
with the accident of human sinfulness. The image of the
Lamb of God exists eternally within the Divine nature and
is revealed to men through the organic wholeness of the
life of the Incarnate Son of God—His birth, His temptation, His suffering, His death and resurrection, His
continuing life in His Body, the Church. Repeatedly,
cyclically, dramatically, the Passion of the Son of God is
re-enacted for us men and for our salvation, here on
earth, within the events of our common life.

Deep in the heart of the Greek is the memory of his
people's constant struggle for freedom and it is not
surprising that he should identify the Passion of his
nation with the Passion of the Christ. In so doing he
reaches out towards the Christus-Victor theme which
was exploited at so early a period by the Fathers of the
Eastern Church. Christ through death and resurrection had won a great victory over Satan and all his
hosts and the way was open to all his followers to share in
His triumph. It might involve suffering and struggle
comparable to His but the ultimate victory was assured.
It is something of this feeling which pervades the epic

stories of the heroic struggles for liberty since the Greek War of Liberation began in 1821. The hero is the representative of the Christ. He may suffer, he may die: his people may suffer and die with him. But victory and resurrection are assured in the name of the Christ who died and rose again on behalf of His own.

There are obvious dangers in such a conception. The association of the Christ-figure with acts of violence, with the encouragement of armed warfare and of leadership into battle in Kazantzakis's novel is bound to raise questions. Yet Manolios himself is never guilty of violence or vengefulness and there must be a place in religion for the notes of judgment and the conquest of evil. What Manolios did he did on behalf of suffering women and children and starving men. He saw the Christ suffering in the experiences of His followers and his very identification with the people of the mountain was bound to involve the championing of their cause. In a story of this kind, the parallels must not be pressed too far and in spite of certain clear incompatibilities the general impression left upon the reader by the character of Manolios is that it is not unworthy of the Christ he was elected to represent.

The highest value of this story is to be found in the vivid picture it gives of the Greek view of life, and in particular of the virtue and influence of the Passion of Christ within the organic wholeness in which life consists. No part of the created order is unrelated to his incarnate life and atoning death. In the cycle of nature they are symbolically represented: in the histories of nations they are openly re-enacted: in the careers of chosen individuals they are perpetuated and reinforced. In the travail of the ages Christ is for ever re-crucified. In the sufferings of the innocent He is for ever in agony. But in this travail and through these sufferings the process of salvation is continually carried forward. The Lamb of God is for ever bearing away the sins of the world.

CHAPTER 5

THE FRIEND LAYS DOWN HIS LIFE

OF ALL the creative achievements of contemporary novelists, none is more impressive than William Faulkner's saga of Yoknapatawpha County in his native Mississippi. The county itself is imaginary, and the stories range over a period of time extending beyond the author's own actual experience. But the sights and sounds so brilliantly evoked through the novels, are the scenes and voices which belong to Oxford and Jefferson and the life of the rural South. No contemporary novelist has kept himself so firmly attached to one particular geographical environment and one critic has even compared him to Antaeus, whose phenomenal strength only deserted him when he lost contact with his mother earth. Faulkner has every right to be regarded as *the* novelist of the American South, and his unique contribution to the world of literature was recognised in 1950 by the award of the Nobel Prize.

In his acceptance speech, on this occasion, Faulkner gave his audience a brief glimpse of the faith by which his own life and work are now determined. (Whether this has always been the case is, perhaps, another matter.) He referred to the " old verities and truths of the heart " —" love and honour, and pity and pride, and compassion and sacrifice." Only these are worth writing about. To write of other things is simply to stand in the midst of the human situation, watching its end. But, Faulkner declared, in words which have become famous, " I decline to accept the end of man ... I believe that man will not merely endure: he will prevail. He is immortal, not because he alone among creatures has an inexhaustible voice, but because he has a soul, a spirit capable of compassion and sacrifice and endurance. The poet's, the writer's duty is to write about these things."

A second fascinating insight into his conception of the novelist's task, may be gained from the record of Faulkner's conversation with his interviewer in the volume, *Writers at Work* (1958). " The aim of every artist," he says, " is to arrest motion, which is life, by artificial means and hold it fixed so that a hundred years later, when a stranger looks at it, it moves again since it is life. Since man is mortal, the only immortality possible for him is to leave something behind him which is immortal, since it will always move. Not moral problems, not metaphysical problems constitute the artist's essential business. Rather he must be concerned with the creation of believable people in credible moving situations." To this idea of life as movement, he recurs again and again. And few would deny that Faulkner himself has succeeded in an astonishing way in creating the sense of movement in his books. The direction and the end of the movement may not always be clear, but the intensity of the movement itself is rarely in question. " Life is motion," is a summary expression of Faulkner's understanding of human existence.

By holding together these two speeches of self-revelation, we gain a picture of a writer who is attempting to create a series of moving situations within which authentic people struggle to express themselves in compassion, in sacrifice and in endurance. In the main he has done this by grasping the imaginary life of Yoknapatawpha County in his prose and allowing it to reveal the old universal truths about which he wants to write. But in one major instance he has moved away from his native earth, and has embraced instead the war-torn soil of a land across the seas. In place of the ordinary day-to-day human experience of typical characters in the Deep South—experience which may indeed contain fleeting references to larger symbolic themes—he gives us an altogether strange, critical, tragic crystallisation of human experience, which is quite manifestly related to the central event of the Christian faith. Sacrifice, compassion, endurance, are most movingly expressed through a narrative which keeps step with the journey from Galilee to Jerusalem, though, in point of fact, the setting is the France of the later part of the 1914-18 war.

A Fable is thus very different from Faulkner's other stories though the basic concern for old, universal truths remains the same. He had worked for nine years on the book before it appeared in 1955, but its ground pattern may be traced back to an even earlier period. For as Nathan Scott has pointed out in his interesting essay entitled, *William Faulkner's Passion Week of the Heart,** it was at the very beginning of his career, in the novel *Mosquitoes*, that he made one of his characters define, as

* In the symposium *The Tragic Vision and the Christian Faith.*

the highest mark of genius in the arts, the creation of a
" Passion Week of the Heart." Certainly the framework
of *A Fable* is the Passion Story of the Gospels, and
although there is much that is obscure, perplexing and
ambiguous in the working out of the story, it is possible
to claim that we have in this book the most ambitious
attempt by any contemporary novelist to bring the
Christian myth or allegory or history—however we may
care to describe it—into the very texture of the life of
twentieth-century man.

Since its appearance, *A Fable* has received the most
varied critical appraisals. In the eyes of some, it is the
author's masterpiece: for others it is " an abominable
failure." To some it is the most Christian of his novels:
to others it is sheer blasphemy. Delmore Schwartz can
describe it as, " A unique fulfilment of Faulkner's genius,
which gives a luminous new meaning to his work as a
whole." John McCormick sums up his impressions by
saying that, " The net effect is that of a film-scenario of
Passion Week collaborated upon by Matthew, Mark,
Luke and Dostoievsky." All of which shows that there
is no possibility of passing judgment easily on a very
complex work of art. Let us instead try to give a brief
sketch of the book itself and note some of its main
features.

II

The chapter titles are simply the names of the days of
the week with the exception of the final chapter which is

called " To-morrow." We begin with " Wednesday," for
it was in Wednesday that the French regiment which had
mutinied on the Western Front some time in the spring
of 1918 was being brought back behind the lines for trial.
The scene in the city, from which much of the original
regiment had been raised, is vividly described. The
people had heard the news only on the Tuesday, but they
were out long before dawn to await the strange procession.
First came the car containing three generals—British,
American and French—who would sit in judgment on
their fellow-men. Then came the regiment itself. Herded
together in lorries, sullen, impassive, the men were being
hurried forward to their unknown doom. Finally, a little
behind the rest, came a single lorry, similar to the others
except for its cargo. For whereas the others had been
filled to capacity, this one carried only thirteen men.
They belonged to the same regiment, but their general
deportment was strangely unlike that of their fellows. And
four of the thirteen were quite clearly foreigners, men maybe from some far-off mountainous district who were unfamiliar with the sights of city life. And even amongst
the four, one stood out in lonely distinction, a corporal,
" with an alien face like all the other twelve, a mountain
peasant's face like the last three, a little younger than
several of them, looking down at the fleeing sea of eyes
and gaped mouths and fists, with the same watchfulness
as the other twelve, but with neither the bafflement nor
the concern—a face merely interested, attentive and calm,
with something else in it which none of the others had: a
comprehension, understanding, utterly free of compassion,
as if he had already anticipated without censure or pity,

the uproar which rose and paced and followed the lorry as it sped on."

As this final lorry reached the Place de Ville, where the soldiers were to be interned, it passed the three generals who, having reached their own destination, had turned to watch the convoy come in. And in that fleeting moment the eyes of the corporal met those of the French generalissimo. Something passed between them in the brief encounter. But it was only for a moment. All had now been brought to their places to await judgment and silence descended once again upon the city square.

Through his opening chapter Faulkner has introduced us to the critical situation as it existed on Wednesday morning. The corporal and his followers, who had somehow been the ringleaders of the mutiny: the largely impassive and uncomprehending regiment: the generalissimo who is in some curious way related to the corporal— all these are intimately concerned with the temporary cessation of hostilities on a particular sector of the Front. But now that the basic situation has been defined, Faulkner proceeds to describe at length the events leading up to it, and because it is often far from easy to determine the precise significance of these events, I shall pick out the five main groups of characters involved, and try to show how they are related to one another.

First there is a group of four generals. Of these the least important is the German general, flown over during the lull to open negotiations, but so completely hidebound by the rules of war that his mission ends in utter futility. General Gragnon, the commander of the mutinous division, represents soldierly virtues at their best. He does not seek security or promotion but, Stoic-fashion, holds to his duty regardless of the consequences. When the division mutinies he demands that all shall be executed, but instead he is himself condemned to this fate. Maintaining his soldierly integrity to the end, and refusing to accept the false death that authority decrees, he is brutally maltreated and shot by three American soldiers hired for the job. Most important, however, are the generalissimo and the quartermaster-general, and a considerable part of the novel is devoted to the telling of their story.

The generalissimo's career has been altogether extra-ordinary. Beginning with every advantage of birth, influence and training, he went straight from his gradu-ation at the military academy to lonely outposts in French colonial territories. There, strange things befell him. He learned, for example, that ordinary man can be a pawn in the game of any high officials: he learned that woman can be used and cast aside though her offspring may still have to be accounted for. Actually, the story reveals, it was the generalissimo's adulterous association with a beautiful hill-country woman that produced the son who was later to appear as the corporal in the silent revolution. It was only after many years spent in far-away lonely places that the general had been recalled in his country's hour of supreme need to shoulder the task of becoming its saviour and deliverer.

The quartermaster-general figures less prominently than the generalissimo, but he has been his friend from the beginning, and serves as an interpreter of his motives and character. He follows him, supports him, becomes his chief aide, and sees the war through to its close. But in his heart he knows that it has all been a betrayal. At the end of the story he emerges for a brief moment in symbolic repentance, and regains a measure of acceptance amongst men through suffering and tears.

The second group consists of three women—Marya, Marthe and Magda. Magda appears at the beginning of the story, when she is seen watching the corporal and his friends going forward to their doom: Marya and Marthe appear at the end, serene in their confidence that their brother's work has not been in vain. In between, their story is unravelled: how Marya and Marthe, having travelled across Europe had settled on a farm in France: and how their farm was in the very centre of the battle-area: and how the brother had come into touch with a girl of the streets, Magda, in Marseilles, and how she had joined the other two during the period of crisis, and then had returned to her labours for the sake of a widowed grandmother. They are finally allowed to receive the dead body of the corporal and to bury it on the farm. But the renewal of hostilities brings a shell into the burying-place and the body disappears only to re-appear by an ironic set of circumstances, in such a manner as to gain the final place of honour in the tomb of the unknown warrior in Paris.

A third group, the least significant perhaps in the story, are officers and men of a Royal Flying Corps camp, concerned with the task of giving the negotiating German general safe passage into the Allied lines. Faulkner had a direct interest in aviation in the First World War and he uses this to portray the career of a young Jewish officer, Levine, who, without knowing what was happening, became involved in the operation. It is a clever psychological study of a young man's disillusionment, not only with the way the war was being conducted on the field, but also with the attitudes of the women, including his mother, who are supporting the war efforts at home. Ultimately he loses his grip and determination and takes the easy way out of self-inflicted death.

The fourth group is in some ways the most mysterious, and yet the most fascinating of all. The central figure is a runner on the British lines, who, because of his compelling desire to regain a true identification with his fellow-men, had employed a grotesque means, while on leave, of renouncing his officer's status. He holds an altogether significant place in the working out of the drama, and appears in the final scene of the book as a figure of triumph. With him are a Cockney sentry who, we learn, had originally been a horse-groom, a Negro preacher and his grandson. These are all involved in the war situation, but in order to give us the background of the parts they play, Faulkner brings in a long story which might almost be regarded as a fable within the larger fable.

It is the story of a fabulous horse and its groom who went out together from Newmarket in 1912. The horse had been sold to a wealthy buyer but its link with its groom was so close that it was arranged for both to go together. After a brief period in the service of its Argentinian owner, it was purchased by a wealthy American who kept stables in Kentucky and had a groom, a Negro, who was also a preacher on Sunday. At New

Orleans the horse and its groom were met by the Negro and his grandson, and the strange quartet set off on the journey to Kentucky.

On the way, however, a bridge over which the rail-track ran, collapsed, and the van containing the horse and its attendants plunged into the river below. Yet, although the horse was badly injured, the ingenuity of the groom succeeded in mending its broken thigh and starting it on a fantastic career of winning races all over the back-country of the Middle West. For sixteen months the quartet evaded every attempt of the authorities to capture them, and when at length the chase was up the groom shot the horse through the head rather than allow it to be taken away to the stud for breeding purposes. Thereafter, with the advent of war, the groom finds his way into the British Army, and works out a scheme by which he becomes beneficiary of the life-insurance policies of the whole battalion in which he serves. The Negro preacher and his grandson become the agents of a wealthy American woman in establishing an organisation in Paris for the promotion of international good will.

The runner, as it happens, serves in the same battalion as the groom and has long been mystified by him. It is only finally on a visit to Paris, where he meets the preacher and hears the full story, that he commits himself to that faith of which the horse had been the central symbol.

The horse had endured its passion, but it had continued to run. He, the runner in name, now becomes a true runner on behalf of the new order which the corporal and his followers represent. He returns to the Front and prevails upon his fellow soldiers to go out into no-man's land in a supreme gesture of reconciliation towards the enemy. Even the groom who has apostatized from his original faith, and been swallowed up in scepticism and greed, is driven forward within the despairing surge towards a common humanity. But at the very moment when hand might have touched hand, the truce breaks, the artillery barrage begins again, and all are engulfed in a new passion of fire. Only the runner emerges alive to continue on his career of running, though he now retains only a sorely stricken and mutilated image of his original humanity.

But the runner's activities have been motivated not simply by his involvement with the strange brotherhood of groom and Baptist preacher and grandson, but also by his contacts with the corporal and his followers. As a runner he has had unusual opportunities of meeting them, and his ultimate faith is directly related to the mission they are seeking to fulfil. And clearly it is this fifth group containing the corporal and the twelve, which is all important in the development of the Passion Week theme.

As a whole the group remains in the shadows. We are told that for months they have been moving freely in the allied lines and have even taken opportunities of going up and down on the German side of the Front. Little is known however of the precise nature of their activities until the moment of crisis arrives. Then that which they have been engineering actually comes to pass. The events follow one another in roughly the same sequence as those of the original Passion Week. The chief exception is the long process of temptation to which the corporal is subjected first at the hands of the generalissimo, and then through the ministrations of the chaplain-priest (though these could be regarded as portraying, in some measure, the struggles of Gethsemane). Aside from this, however, there is the betrayal by a Judas-figure, the denial by a Peter-figure, a last supper, a vivid scene with two malefactors, and a crucifixion scene, in which the corporal and the two evil men are tied up to posts and shot. Finally, the women are allowed to take the body away and to bury it in the home-farm.

The last chapter of the story is entitled, " To-morrow." It relates first a strange episode of twelve soldiers and their sergeant being sent to Verdun to collect a body from one of the great vaults of the dead, and after a series of raucous adventures, actually bringing back the body of the dead corporal for interment in the place of honour in the nation's capital. Next it tells of the visit of the runner, together with the old quartermaster-general, to the women on the farm, and of the renewal of repentance and faith in the home of simple devotion. Finally, we are given a glimpse of the generalissimo's funeral, disturbed by the runner's daring and defiant interruption. He narrowly escapes lynching by the crowd, and takes his leave of the reader, lying on the gutter of a small cul-de-sac, but still laughing (running, as it were, in spirit), and crying out, " I'm not going to die. Never."

III

The setting of Faulkner's Passion Story is peculiarly significant. One would have expected him to fasten upon

some unusual situation in his own native Mississippi—
either in the time of the Civil War, or in the more recent
period of the intensifying of race tensions. But instead he
transfers his interest to the most grim and ghastly setting
of the twentieth century—the theatre of war in France
during the 1914-18 conflict. The novel was begun in
December, 1944, before Hiroshima, and it is possible
that if Faulkner were writing to-day the areas devastated
by atomic warfare might give him an even more impressive staging for his drama. Be that as it may, it remains true that before the perils of atomic radiation were
let loose, no more horrible example of the nature of
modern warfare had been seen than the two opposing
Fronts swaying backwards and forwards in Flanders for
four years, with the attendant destruction of virtually
everything that makes life outwardly worth while.

Through the constant shelling and trench-digging the
very earth itself had become a corpse. There is a moving
scene when the guns begin again after the brief armistice.
The three women and the husband have returned to the
farm " which had been the life of the brother, and which
was to have been his some day." The husband looks out
over the ruined farm, " his land ": he sinks into an un-
easy sleep, crying out from time to time, " The farm. The
land ": and then suddenly, they are all aroused as the
shelling begins, and they run stumbling out to a tre-
mendous crater for protection, " the husband crying
steadily, in a voice as thin and constant as a cicada's:
" The land. The land. The land." Nature itself lies
in ruins because of Man's utter folly.

It is in the chapter entitled " To-morrow," however,

that Faulkner pours out his feelings about the rape of the earth. The sergeant in the lorry going to Verdun, to collect the body for interment in Paris, watches the ruined and slain land unfold—" the corpse of earth, some of which, its soil soured forever with cordite and human blood and anguish, would never live again, as though not only abandoned by man but repudiated forever by God Himself: the craters, the old trenches and rusted wire, the stripped and blasted trees, the little villages and farms like shattered skulls no longer even recognisable as skulls, already beginning to vanish beneath a fierce rank colourless growth of nourishmentless grass coming not tenderly out of the earth's surface but as though miles and leagues up from Hell itself, as if the Devil himself were trying to hide what man had done to the earth which was his mother."

Such has been the effect of war already. But in another extended passage, Faulkner sees beyond this, to the ghastly possibilities of the future—to a time when man will have abandoned for ever his relationship to land and home and will have become encased in the automobile from which he need never dismount. " Peripatetic, unceasing and long since no longer countable, to die at last at the click of an automatic circuit-breaker on a speedometer dial, and, long since freed of bone and organ and gut, leaving nothing for communal scavenging but a rustling and odourless shell, the shell which he does not get out of because he does not need to, but which presently for a time he will not emerge from because he does not dare because the shell will be his only protection from the hail-like iron refuse from his wars."

In bitter irony, Faulkner depicts the last gigantic wrestling match between two Frankenstein monsters, in the last red and heatless sunset—the nemesis of man's greed and rapacity and violence. This is the environment within which, in this twentieth century, the Passion must be portrayed.

As regards the setting in time, the Week can only be described as an altogether unique time of visitation. What happened on the Western Front in the spring of 1918 was unparalleled, unrepeatable. It took place at springtime and thereby had a link with man's seasons of hope. But in every other way it was a time out of time, a brief period of hours, an almost unreal holding of mankind's breath, a tense moment of quiet between the roaring of the guns. Yet that brief period gathered up into itself the destinies of all manner of representative groups. The rulers and statesmen and all the manifold hierarchies who hold the responsibility for making war: the eternal feminine, the women who love and suffer and seek peace: the black and the white, the Asiatic and the European, the East and the West, the Church and the World: the dumb, patient multitudes of civilians and the seething, moiling, spiritless masses of combatants— all are represented in these fateful hours which determine the destiny of mankind.

Such is the setting in space and time which Faulkner chooses for the enactment of his Passion-drama. Obviously the situation is not entirely without parallel. What happened in first-century Palestine in the very midst of the political struggles and national tensions of that period is constantly in Faulkner's mind. There the

Passion was being played out against a background of imperial wars and national uprisings, the agonies of the meek-spirited, and the uncertainties of the common man. But, he seems to say, if we of the twentieth century are to see the reality and meaning of this same Passion, we must view it within the context of our own crisis, the crisis of total war with the world divided into two opposing halves, each assuming that its own salvation can only be gained through the complete annihilation of the other. Unless the Passion becomes real within the setting of war, war which destroys earth and home and decency and the rhythm of life and mutual respect and the intimacy of human relationships, it has no ultimate bearing upon the human situation.

IV

It is not easy to sketch the wider philosophical system to which *A Fable* belongs. The world in which Faulkner has lived is a world of tension and conflict between races, classes and individuals. Even in the comparative seclusion of Yoknapatawpha County, black and white, the old county families and the new commercial groups, the town and the country, the living order of nature and the dead power of money are at variance. Still more in the wider world outside, he sees the vast struggle between nations, each with its own hierarchy of war-lords whose business it is to see that " the formal orderly shooting of one set of men by another wearing the same uniform " goes on: the struggle between rival financial interests with an occasional Mammon's David ringing a " Mammon's Goliath's brazen, invincible unregenerate skull." The uniform and the dollar—these Faulkner seems to say are the great corrupters of human life. Man will sell his birthright in the human race for the sake of wearing candy-stripes on his uniform: he will barter his dignity as an individual for the privilege of a larger share in the vast impersonal financial empire which the world's banks sustain.

Where then, within this age-long conflict, can true values be found? If the whole world is caught up in the grim struggle for money, and in the still grimmer alternatives of a " cold " or " hot " war, how shall man endure, let alone prevail? Faulkner is not prepared to accept any facile answer to these questions. But he believes that there have been in the past, and can still be in the present, individual manifestations of such compassion and sacrifice as are capable of redeeming the situation. In them and through them man becomes truly man, and those who accept and believe, regain their birthright within the human race.

The question of historicity, in the sense of whether such and such an individual actually lived in a particular period, and such and such an event actually happened in the world of space and time, troubles Faulkner but little. This inquiry is not his business. His concern is to meditate upon the great stories of the past and to create his own stories in the present. In his Paris interview he refers to these stories of the past as " allegories," though I doubt if any precise significance should be attached to the use of this particular word. They are stories about representative individuals, in representative situations, and as such, Faulkner says, they are the charts against which man can measure himself and learn to know what he is. They reveal, in an overpowering way, the existence in human life of courage and compassion and sacrifice and hope. They show, in other words, that amidst all within history and experience that would lead us to despair of the human race, there are matchless examples of the contrary embedded in the world's literatures, and it is by those examples that man can still set his course and *run* towards his true goal.

Amidst these " matchless examples," Faulkner clearly gives a high place of honour to the Passion Story of the Gospels. He deliberately chooses it from amongst other noble stories of the past to provide the ground-plan of his novel, and although there is no reason to suggest that he regards it as a unique illustration of human sacrificial action, he must consider it the most impressive framework within which to set his own twentieth century creation. It reveals " suffering and sacrifice, and the promise of hope," and when man sees that, he knows that true victory within the human situation is at least not impossible.

Moreover, Faulkner is careful to distinguish the true victory of faith from the false confidence which inflates the rulers of this world. There is a striking similarity at first sight between his own acceptance speech at Stockholm and parts of the generalissimo's speech to the corporal in the temptation-scene. But, within its wider context, it becomes clear that the generalissimo is committing himself to a hollow confidence in man's power to endure by

means of his own dogged struggle against adverse circumstances, and by his own capacity to remain in control
of all the fabrications of his own inventive genius. In other
words, in the general's view, natural man, predatory
man, domineering man, superman, will endure. But
this to Faulkner is blasphemy. Only moral man, com-
passionate man, sacrificial man, will endure and prevail.
In spite of all that seems to deny such a faith and hope, it
is clearly the purpose of *A Fable* to confirm that this is
indeed so.

But such a faith can neither be lightly gained nor
easily retained. The man of faith is essentially the
runner, the man who neither drifts nor sits but runs. As
critics have pointed out, the theme of running is central
to the novel. The runner appears at an early stage and
remains to the end. His is an amazing career. Beginning
with certain natural advantages, he renounces them in
order, as it were, to start again from scratch. He then
advances to his true moral stature, partly through his
spasmodic contacts with the corporal and his group, but
more particularly through his encounter with the Negro
preacher and through his subsequent initiation into the
story of the fabulous horse. For the altogether significant
characteristic of the horse was its ability to go on running.
Through all vicissitudes, even through injury and dis-
ability, it continued to race and to win. Through
devotion to the horse, the symbol of faith, men of opposite
types and traditions found a common faith and brotherhood. And through hearing the story the runner gained
the necessary courage to return to the Front and to lead
men out in a crusade of faith which, while it seemed to

fail, left him in possession of a burning confidence which nothing could quench.

The final appearances of the runner are full of interest. He is now little more than half a man physically: he must use crutches: but he still contrives to run. His devotion has now been given to that for which the corporal lived and died, and even when prevented from running, he can still laugh, not the laughter of mockery or levity, but the gay running laughter of faith which believes that nothing can finally defeat compassion and suffering and love. At the beginning of Passion Week, the runner had found himself saying, " It's not that we didn't believe; it's that we couldn't, didn't know how any more. That's the most terrible thing they have done to us." On Wednesday night in the company of the Negro preacher, he could say, " Maybe what I need is to have to meet somebody. To believe. Not in anything, just to believe." And on Thursday belief becomes strong through action, and there is, henceforward, no turning back. Himself baptized with the fire of suffering, he yet goes forward to bear witness to the world that faith and hope and love are the things which endure for ever.

Can this philosophy of Faulkner's in any way be called a theology? Outwardly there is little reference to God, or to the Christ of history, or even to the traditional doctrines of theism. Moreover, there are ironical statements about institutional religion and there is the relentless description of the chaplain-priest, first selling his soul and then taking his own life. Yet it is hard to write Faulkner off as a humanist pure and simple or as an anti-religious sceptic. For if anything is certain it is that

Faulkner has no confidence in man as he exists in his merely natural state, or as he seeks to extend his dominion over the world by merely natural agencies. The all-important thing is the development of a moral conscious-ness, and nothing is more powerful to produce this than a story of courage and faith and sacrifice. But what, may we ask, creates either the deed or the story? If it is not a natural agency, it must, in some sense, be a more than natural agency, a spiritual agency. And as soon as we speak of the spirit, the door is open to a theological interpretation of the universe and of human existence.

Faulkner certainly exalts the attitude of semi-religious devotion exemplified by the Baptist preacher and the Masonic groom. He finds a place for the mysterious, as in the strange testimonies of the three officers that they have known the corporal at three quite separate places within the period 1914-1917, though each affirms that he saw him die. To this the supreme commander replies in bitter contempt, " one of our Allies' officers . . . saw him slain . . . another buried him . . . so all that remains for us is to witness his resurrection." Delmore Schwartz may be justified in his comment that, " the officers' certainty that the corporal has died, and returned among the living three times, is their unwitting intuitive expression of the necessity of such a being as Christ or the corporal every day, every week, every year. His perpetual death and return is a perpetual necessity."

It is true that Faulkner is not prepared to go beyond the suggestion of mystery and the possible legitimacy of religious myths as agents of living faith. But at least it would be unfair to label him anti-supernaturalist, and his book leaves the way open to us to believe that the love and compassion which he so ardently desires for the world can only be produced, whether in life or in literature, by a spirit that is more than human, the Spirit of the Living God Himself.

V

I have tried to sketch the background in space and time and the general estimate of man which Faulkner's novel contains. I want finally to look at the picture of the corporal himself and try to understand his significance within the novelist's view of the total human situation.

Faulkner's use of Biblical concepts and even language is exceedingly skilful. Again and again we are reminded irresistibly of a Biblical parallel, and yet it is rarely a question of a merely literal reproduction. What is told of the birth and early life of the corporal, for example, is suggestive without becoming a direct parallel. Born in the hill-country out of wedlock, the son of a man who was in course of time to be the leader of the world's most powerful army (in very truth the Prince of the World), the boy was brought by his sisters out of obscurity into the midst of civilisation, and would, in the normal course of events, have taken possession of the farm which was his rightful inheritance.

But other forces were moving in his world. The war comes, he joins the forces and takes his place at once in the great struggle. Then the strange thing begins to happen about which we are told little, except that he becomes a corporal and somehow gathered around him a motley band of like-minded men. And this group moved about freely within the Allied lines, and even penetrated to the other side of the great divide. "Not only were the foreign corporal and his strange conglomerate squad known personally to every private in those three divisions, but for over two years now the thirteen men— the obscure corporal whose name few knew and even they could not pronounce it, whose very presence in the regiment, along with that of the other three apparently of the same Middle-European nationality, was an enigma, since none of them seemed to have any history at all beyond the day when they had appeared, material-ised seemingly out of nowhere and nothingness in the quartermaster's store-room where they had been issued uniforms and equipment, and the nine others who were authentic and, until this morning, unimpeachable Frenchmen and French soldiers, had been spending their leaves and furloughs for two years now among the combat-troop rest-billets not only throughout the entire French Army zone, but the American and the British ones too, sometimes individually, but usually as the intact squad—the entire thirteen, three of whom couldn't even speak French, visiting for days and sometimes weeks at a time, not only among French troops, but American and British too "; And during three of their two-week leave periods, " the entire squad had vanished from France itself, vanished one night with their passes and trans-port, and ration-warrants from their rest-billets, and re-appeared one morning two weeks later in ranks again— monstrous and incredible, since there was but one place

114

on earth in almost four years now where thirteen men in uniform could have gone without having their papers stamped, needing no papers at all in fact, only darkness and a pair of wire-cutters."

What exactly they did, what they said in their wanderings, we can only surmise. The fact remains that when the day of crisis came, the incredible thing happened: a whole division remanded, and although the enemy was well aware that it was being withdrawn as a complete unit from the trenches, he made no attempt to take advantage of the situation, but allowed peace for a few brief hours to descend upon the desolate and desecrated theatre of war.

In effect the corporal has hitherto been assuming the incognito of Kierkegaard's Christ. It is only the events of the Passion Week that reveal him in his true nature, and by these his message and ministry must be judged. Everything that happens to him, he meets with strength, with dignity, and with fortitude. We see him at the window of the cell, fearless, controlled, while the crowd is surging forward in the square below like a mountainous wave of the sea. We see him presiding at the incongruous last supper, with Polchek, the traitor, proposing the toast to " Peace "—" Haven't we finally got what we've all been working for for four years now? "—and Pierre Bouc, anguished, despairing, unable to drink the toast and clutching at the opportunity of denying his identity with the group, when a way of escape suddenly appears. We see him rising from supper to appear before the generalissimo and leaving behind the dirty, unshaven, band, " Harassed, but absolute, one in whatever it was—

not trust exactly, not dependence: perhaps just one-ness, singleness."

The longest appearance of the corporal is in the great temptation scene. Here at last the real issue is joined. The prince of this world confronts the prince of peace whom he has begotten in such ironical circumstances. He first offers him liberty—the chance to leave behind everything in war-scarred Europe and to disappear into obscurity in the Western world. The corporal scorns to desert his comrades. He then offers to execute Polchek in his stead, or if he will not accept that, to release Polchek with him. And the reply comes back, " There are still that ten." Yet again the general offers to make him his ally and confederate in setting up a world kingdom—mundane power and spiritual leadership united in a magnificent harmonious empire. And again he rejects the proposal with scorn. Finally, the tempter plays his last card. All that a man hath will he give in exchange for his life. Take life.

" Recant, confess, say you were wrong: that what you led was—led? You led nothing: you simply participated —an attack which failed to advance. Take life from me; ask mercy and accept it. I can give it even for a military failure." And the corporal chooses death, believing that nothing but his death, the symbol and the pledge of final integrity—can save mankind.

With the great temptation passed, the story moves rapidly to its climax. The corporal is bundled into a cell where he finds two degraded creatures, brilliantly described by the novelist: Lapin, to whom thieving is second nature, and continues with him even in the condemned cell: Horse, whose only desire is to get to Paris with all that it implies. They have been condemned for a cold-blooded murder and are to be executed publicly in order that justice may be seen to have been done. Next morning, all three are taken out to the square, bound with cords to posts, and the volley from the rifles of twenty soldiers does the rest. The corporal's last words are addressed to the wretched man who is crying " Paris " in a voice that is, " hoarse, and wet and urgent." " It's all right. We're going to wait. We won't go without you." And in the last view we have of him, he is strangely crowned with thorns.

" The corporal's post may have been flawed or even rotten because, although the volley merely cut cleanly the cords binding Lapin and the third man to theirs, so that their bodies slumped at the foot of each post, the corporal's body, post bonds and all, went over backward as one intact unit, on to the edge of the rubbish-filled trench behind it; when the sergeant-major, the pistol still smoking faintly in his hand, moved from Lapin to the corporal, he found that the plunge of the post had jammed it and its burden too into a tangled mass of old barbed wire, a strand of which had looped up and around the top of the post and the man's head as though to assoil them both in one unbroken continuation of the fall, into the anonymity of the earth."

The story of the entombment and of the disappearance of the body is beautifully told but there is no suggestion of actual resurrection. All that remains is the comedy of " To-morrow." The tragedy of Friday is followed by a comic reversal in which man's most careful plans are brought to nought and the body of the one who was rejected by men is entombed in the shrine of highest honour. And again, as Marya is united with the disfigured runner in a moment of common devotion, they find themselves laughing, " strong and steady and completely " their eyes meeting in, " full and calm and unpitying joy." There may be no formal place for resurrection, but the conclusion of the story leaves no excuse for despair. Rather the meek and broken of the earth are running and laughing and dancing with hope because one man was found who proved faithful to the end and worthy to become the saviour of mankind.

Judgments of this fascinating, baffling and finally mysterious novel, will continue to differ. It is heretical—but virtually all the poets who have written about the Christian theme have bordered on heresy. It is ambiguous—but how can there be faith unless there is ambiguity? But whatever it is, it is not trivial or hollow. It comes to grips with the two great juggernaut monsters which are threatening the very survival of the human race—War and Mammon. It claims that they will yet be overcome by integrity and sacrifice and indomitable hope. Such a faith may be too this-worldly, too man-centred. At least it leaves open the door to a running faith* which finds such a man only in the story of the God-Man, who for the joy that was set before Him, endured the cross, despising the shame, and is now set down at the right hand of the throne of God.

* Hebrews 12. vv. 1.

CHAPTER 6

THE INSOLUBLE PARADOX

" If, when we finish reading *Billy Budd*, we are left with questions which we feel have been raised but not answered, if so to speak the equation has not come out to a finite number, as in a work of art it should, this is not due to any lack of talent on Melville's part, but to the insolubility of the religious paradox in aesthetic terms." w. h. auden.

This is Mr. Auden's final estimate of *Billy Budd*. But what does he mean by the " religious paradox "? In a subsequent expansion of this phrase Mr. Auden looks first at the whole career of the Christ and comments on the paradox involved in his sinlessness.* He then considers the suffering and the crucifixion. The suffering, he says, must at one and the same time be willed *and* not willed. If it seems entirely against the will of the sufferer he becomes pathetic: if it seems entirely the result of his own actions, he becomes tragic. Pathos involves elements of humiliation: tragedy involves elements of pride. But neither unwilling humiliation nor willed pride befit the Christ-figure.

Again so far as the crucifixion is concerned the hero must be shown as failing in a worldly sense, that is as

* *The Enchafed Flood.* 119 *f.*

coming into collision with the law of this world. Otherwise his sinlessness could be regarded simply as the worldly prudence which avoids clashes with the settled order. On the other hand worldly failure is not in itself a guarantee of supernatural character: as Auden remarks, the crucified Christ is flanked by two crucified thieves.

To attempt then to represent the passion of Christ *directly* as a work of art is to invite failure. It can only be represented obliquely, indirectly, above all paradoxically. Whenever the painter, for example, has tried to give a direct representation of the suffering Christ or of the heroic Christ or of the submissive Christ or of the impassive Christ, the result has never been more than a half-truth. Unless the painter or the sculptor can give some impression of the tension between two aspects of the redemptive action, unless he can, in fact, give us a vivid sense of the great *paradox* involved in the work of a Christ-figure he falls short of Christian truth. And to present such a tension or paradox in aesthetic terms is as difficult as any task can be. A Fra Angelico can paint a Crucifixion scene in which the bodily beauty of the Christ is scarcely impaired, where his face is noble and serene and almost passionless, where those who wield the nails and spear perform the task as a strange duty rather than as a harsh atrocity. A Grunewald can show the Christ of Calvary as brutally mutilated, with no beauty that we should desire him, not only rejected by men but tortured, lacerated, desecrated by men, a figure subjected to the worst extremes of sadism of which the human race is capable. Each of these representations is in itself a heresy and though heresies may at times be necessary in order to recall us to the central paradox, it is better that the paradox should as far as possible be expressed within the work of art itself.

What the plastic arts by their very nature find it difficult to do, the dynamic arts can more readily accomplish. The musician and the story-teller can set two contrasting elements in such close juxtaposition that the paradox can make an overwhelming impression upon the listener or the reader. This is for example supremely the case in Bach's Passion Music. In a way that had never been done before Bach made the shouts of the crowd terrifying, fanatical, almost insane. Yet in immediate contrast came music of indescribable tenderness and victorious calm. In and through the passage between the polar opposites the central paradox comes near to aesthetic realisation.

And the same is true of the novelist's art. Through his story he can show us the behaviour of a man whose path leads all the time through the jaws of the supreme antimonies—God and Man, Heaven and Earth, Eternity and Time, the Holy and the Demonic, Freedom and Necessity, the One and the Many. The hero gathers up into himself one or more of these contrasts and becomes the battle ground of the conflict until some temporary resolution is found. But no resolution in aesthetic terms can be final just as no resolution in ethical terms can be. We continue to frame our theories of atonement and our doctrines of reconciliation. None is final in its expression. Each can only try to throw a shaft of light upon the problem which has we believe been brought to a central and determinative solution in the unique *activity* of a unique Person but which defies all attempts to solve it completely in any other way.

II

Can we then categorise in any simple way the contributions which the four novelists whose works we have examined have made to the solution of the paradox? Looking first at the group as a whole it is of interest that whereas two belong to the European and Catholic tradition, a tradition which has always treasured the sacramental, the historically continuous, the settled social structure, the unchanging symbolic forms of community life, the other two belong to the American and Reformed experience, an experience which has always related itself to the frontier, to a tension between the old and the new, to the historically revolutionary, to changing social patterns, to the dynamic potentialities of verbal communication. Christendom itself reveals the paradoxical character of the total human witness to the Christ.

Or again from another point of view whereas two of our writers focus their attention upon problems of individual psychology, the other two are far more concerned with social evils and social remedies. Mauriac and Melville portray a severely limited number of individual personalities, their struggles in their own hearts, their struggles in their relationships with one another, their struggles to discover meaning in the total mystery of things. On the other hand Kazantzakis and Faulkner paint on an exceedingly broad canvas, exposing to our view the clashes between nations and tribes and cultures, the tragic incidence of famine, pestilence and homelessness, the struggles of social groups to attain stability, significance and wholeness within a world which so often seems hostile and meaningless. The very witness to the Christ given by each pair points up the paradox inherent in the relation between the individual and the social, between personal salvation and social integration.

But the paradox may also be discerned when we look at each individual story. Mauriac's central concern is to portray a Christ-figure in terms of *disinterested love*. Xavier has no ambitions of his own. His overmastering desire is to give himself completely to anyone and everyone who needs his help. Yet it is immediately evident that he cannot do this without arousing possessiveness, even hatred in those whom he longs to serve. Moreover the love which is designed for all only becomes intense and real as it is channelled towards the particular individual who seems to be predestined to cross its path. Still further the free and spontaneous outpouring of devotion is quickly drawn into the complex pattern of a total drama of salvation so that freedom to love and necessity to suffer become essential parts of the final paradox of redemption.

Insofar as Mauriac holds fast to the paradox, his story retains its aesthetic impressiveness and its spiritual authenticity. His weakness it may be suggested—and it is the weakness of Catholic theology generally—is to resolve the paradox by some direct break-through of a religious kind. The *deus ex machina*, the undeniably miraculous event, the too-obvious appearance of the

Divine within the earthly form, may seem to have their justification as pointers to the manifestation of an unearthly beauty and to the workings of a supernatural grace, but the intervention may take place at too great a cost. Both aesthetically and spiritually the final effect may be of something unnatural but not supernatural, fascinating but not compelling. The paradox must not be solved by a religious *tour de force* which can be described baldly, literally, almost scientifically. Reality evaporates in such a context.

In a very different way Melville's concern is to portray a Christ-figure in terms of what may be called *innocent love*. Billy Budd is described as The Babe. He is without suspicion, friendly, open, devoid of all self-seeking, with malice towards none. But Melville knows that such a blissful innocence cannot remain unsullied in the midst of a world of evil passions. For some strange reason innocence provokes envy, a simple friendliness draws out hostility, the very ingenuousness of a childlike trust brings into the open the mystery of iniquity. But there is a further paradox. Innocence only advances to full stature as it resists evil and yet this very resistence can have the most tragic consequences. And then the final paradox emerges: Innocent as an angel of God but the angel must hang!

Melville's greatest temptation—and it is the temptation to which much of Reformed theology has succumbed—is to resolve the paradox religiously by assuming that man can enter fully into a subjective apprehension of the inner reconciliation between Father and Son within the divine nature even when the panorama of world events retains its paradoxical character. Billy the innocent one goes forward to his doom but his journey is to some extent unreal seeing that he is already in perfect harmony with the representative of legal justice (" God bless Captain Vere "), and a supernatural atmosphere of calm seems to attend his way. It is not so much the case, as in Mauriac's novel, that the Divine acts miraculously in the world of space and time and thereby resolves the paradox religiously at the expense of the aesthetic. Rather it is that the Divine acts within the inner consciousness of the hero in such a way as to make him impervious to the pressure of outward events. Again the power of the aesthetic representation is lessened by the premature religious resolution.

Kazantzakis's concern may perhaps be described as an attempt to portray a Christ-figure in terms of *universal love*. Manolios has no desire save to live in peace and harmony with the land, with his flock, with his companions, with the villagers, with the refugees, with the whole world. But the same paradox governs the story. His very spirit of compassion brings out the worst in the village Pope, in the elders, above all in the Judas-figure. Moreover the love which moves him to identify himself with the refugees, seeking thereby to draw the two villages together into a common life, seems only to stir up worse hatreds and finally to produce open conflict. And the paradox becomes still more sharply defined when the God of universal compassion is shown as the God of the armies of judgment marching forward to break down and destroy.

Yet in spite of the fact that religious strictures and theological criticisms can readily be applied to Kazantzakis's novel it does succeed in retaining the paradox and thereby preserving the aesthetic appeal to a far greater extent than do the stories of Mauriac and Melville. There is no premature resolution of the conflict. It is true that the episode of the leprous face is somewhat out of character with the rest of the story but the overall picture of Manolios and his companions representing Christ and His Gospel in the midst of a very naughty world is extraordinarily impressive and in the last resort authentically Christian. For it bears witness to death and resurrection, to suffering and release, to sacrifice and new life, to vicarious endurance of hardship and freedom for new adventure as being essential dualities within the wholeness of the Christian faith. The paradox is unresolved but through the very conflict of opposites, man's eyes are lifted up to behold the face of a God of justice and of love.

And much the same judgment may be passed on the work of Faulkner in *A Fable*. Here we find an attempt to describe the fate of a figure who represents nothing more nor less than *reconciling love*. We know little of his character otherwise. He lives and moves for the most part incognito. But around him the destinies of individuals and nations are gathered. This in itself is paradox—that an obscure corporal could be the touchstone of the world's fate.

Religiously, the story is open to every kind of criticism. But when all has been said, this mysterious Christ-figure with his faith that man can be saved and that he is worth saving exercises a strange fascination upon those who are prepared to take him seriously. Faulkner is too fine an artist to attempt any facile resolution of the staggering paradox of man's inhumanity to man and of the suffering of those who love greatly. But he holds tenaciously to the opposites in the belief that those who are willing to yield their imaginations up to a participation in his fable will thereby be purged of lesser loyalties and animosities and be renewed in the spirit of compassion and sacrifice which alone can endure.

III

What then is the conclusion of the whole matter? I have tried to examine the ways in which four great novelists have re-told the story of the Passion within the framework of their own respective traditions and cultures. I have drawn attention to the many ways in which a particular cultural pattern is reflected in the novelist's emphases and interpretations of the one basic story. I have ventured to pass certain judgments on the religious and aesthetic success or failure of each of the novels which we have considered.

In the end it is the story itself which remains. No attempt to re-tell it within any particular context can be finally successful. But the attempt must constantly be made. For some the compelling form may be the simple visual imagery of *The Lamb*: for others it may be the complex verbal imagery of *A Fable*. Some will gain a deeper apprehension of the story through the sustained dramatic excitement of *Christ Re-crucified*, others through the taut economy of *Billy Budd*. But in one way or another the story must be told.

Is not this the supreme need of our own time, especially in the civilisation of the West? We have no central and controlling myth around which the lives of individuals and societies can be re-fashioned. It is comparatively easy to construct psychological prescriptions for the health of the individual and sociological blue-prints for the welfare of society. But valuable as these may be they tend to become doctrinaire and uninspiring, impressive in theory but ineffective in practical application. It is the story which can become both a revelation of reality and an intensely powerful motivating force in individual and corporate life.

It is the faith of the Christian that the record of the Passion, Death and Resurrection of Jesus Christ constitutes such a story. It reveals ultimate reality: it moves man to ultimate commitment. It illuminates the mystery of human estrangements: it points the way forward to final reconciliation. The novelist tries to put the story into the context of a world which we can recognise as our own world. He does not ask us to take it literally. He does ask us to take it seriously for it is out of his own travail that the Passion Story for our own time and condition has been born.